Sherry Glaser

One Woman's
Affectionate
Look at a Relatively
Painful Subject

family
secrets

a fireside book published by
Simon & Schuster

FIRESIDE
Rockefeller Center
1230 Avenue of the Americas
New York, NY 10020

FIRESIDE and colophon are registered trademarks
of Simon & Schuster Inc.

Designed by Elina D. Nudelman

Manufactured in the United States of America

1 3 5 7 9 10 8 6 4 2

Library of Congress Cataloging-in-Publication Data

Glaser, Sherry.
Family secrets : one woman's affectionate
look at a relatively painful subject / Sherry Glaser.
p.   cm.
"A fireside book."
1. Glaser, Sherry—Family.   2. Women dramatists, American—
20th century—Family relationships.   3. Jewish women—United States—
Biography.   4. Jewish families—United States—Drama.   5. Jewish
families—United States.   6. Jews—United States—Drama.   I. Title.
PS3557.L315Z464   1997
812'.54
[B]—DC20   96-42070
                                                               CIP
ISBN 0–684–83023-X

Lyrics on page 71 used by permission of Robyn Samuels.

Let me introduce myself. I'm the one in the family who causes all the trouble. There's one in every family. We each act out in different ways: some steal, some do drugs, some cheat, some lie, and some completely devastate the family by telling the truth about the family. I did all of those things.

Sometimes the person who senses the subtle improprieties in the family or is witness or victim to the gross dysfunctions, tries to speak out. Often such people are ignored or even punished. Sometimes they try to contain it and end up crazy. If they're lucky, they become artists expressing their unresolved emotions on the canvas, piano, or the stage. I find myself on the stage. I believe if everyone wrote a show about their family we would have an epidemic of mental health and a renaissance in play-writing. We would see the most hilarious and agonizing dramas to come across our footlights in a long time.

Family Secrets is a one-person play I wrote with my husband, Greg Howells. It is based on the stories and the people in my family. I have been performing it for seven years, from its inception at a tiny bookstore in San Diego to the prestigious boards of Off Broadway. During the one hour and forty minutes I am on the stage I play Mort, my father; Bev, my mother; Fern, myself at 25; Sandra, myself at 16; and Rose, my grandmother.

I'm a Gemini. I was born on June 7, 1960. I missed the triple sixes by four hours and thirty-seven minutes. I guess I'm blessed. My moon sign is in Scorpio and my rising sign is in Taurus.

The sun sign is the one to which we ascend. Gemini is a mutable (ever changing) air sign. Air represents the aspect of the self that is the mind. Gemini is the sign of the twins. It is ruled by the planet Mercury, characterized by communication and teaching and quick processing. Geminis are usually artists, actors, teachers, or politicians. Some see Gemini as a sign of multiple personalities. For a while it was for me. I could act normal, but I'd experience incredible mood swings, conflicting attitudes in my own psyche that could easily have been diagnosed as schizophrenia. Later, this influence allowed me, as an actor, to slip effortlessly into other people's skins, voices, faces, and feelings, forgetting who I really am.

The moon sign rules one's emotions. Scorpio is a water sign, and water symbolizes the emotions. I've got emotional emotions. Sometimes, like the stinging poisonous creature that governs the sign, they are dark and dangerous secrets. It is the passion of my moon that feeds the unrelenting force of these feelings and keeps the waves coming constantly, whether they are gently rolling over the jetty or mercilessly pounding it into sand.

The rising sign is the way one manifests one's presence on earth, the grounding force in one's life. Taurus is the bull, an earth sign. It is a move-out-of-my-way type of personality. No matter what has gone on in the everyday drama of life, I've had to go to work and get on that stage and spill my guts out. Sometimes it's the last place on earth I want to be, but my ass is sewn on that bull's back. *Yee-haw!*

I love the day I was born. I love the hour and the minute and the family I chose to come to. I believe I came with many lessons to learn in that house and I came with a purpose. I am here to heal my pain, not only from this life, but any others that might have cleaved unto me on my evolutionary journey, which I believe started thousands of years ago.

I was born in the Bronx, the first child to Norm and Shelly Glaser. My first few years were spent in Queens—Jackson Heights, New York. Looking back, I'm filled with a sense of dread that seemed to pervade my infancy and childhood. There, in the garden apartment on 79th Street in Jackson Heights, my childhood fears of death, abandonment, and insecurities about who I was, what I did, how I looked were nurtured like a greedy philodendron because of the perfect coincidences of my family traumas.

The early sixties were surreal—Bermuda shorts and miniskirts, love beads and Nehru jackets. The great rebellion of the hippies and the wail of rock and roll were exploding like great Fourth of July fireworks. The first song I ever learned was the Beatles' "She Loves You." But in Queens, the middle class was strangely subdued. My father took the train to Manhattan every morning at the same time, and my mother . . . comes later.

My father is a mucky-muck. He loves the wheeling and dealing and the style of being a high-powered executive. He's good at it. He is a tax wizard. He likes the real security of numbers, though they are completely abstract to me. He has a business character, so much so that when he is talking business on the phone, his voice and his articulation change. His lips narrow and his r's are more pronounced. He is a powerful man.

He reminds me of a dog. He's not unattractive; in fact, he's quite striking. Six feet three. Thick, black curly hair. He's just sixty and still has only a little gray. His features are strong and his physique is solid from years of basketball and tennis. It's just that he's loyal, loyal as the sky in California is blue. If you're part of his family or someone he cares about, you will have his care and affection and support until you're dead. And he works hard. Ever since I've known him he was up somewhere between five-thirty or six in the morning and at work until six or seven at night.

That was the routine for a man in the fifties and sixties, and my father always went by the rules. Right and wrong are very clear to him. His father, Bob, was a cook at a bar in Manhattan. My grandfather became an alcoholic because he had so much access to booze and not enough self-esteem or education to avoid it. My father, the oldest of three boys (his youngest brother was nineteen years younger than he), took over the role of father. He had a job and he went to night school. He became an accountant. He wanted to become an engineer, but numbers came so easily to him that accounting was the path of least resistance. He met my mother at an engagement party for Simone Goldman. They danced. My father towered over my mother, who is five feet three inches. She had a stiff neck the next morning from looking up at him all night. It was a perfect match.

On February 14, 1959, after he finished serving his country at Fort Dix, my mother and father were married at the Paradise Caterers on the Grand Concourse in the Bronx. By November of '59 my mother was pregnant with me. My father was making only fifty dollars a week, so he went right out and got a hundred-dollar-a-week job. When my brother arrived, he did better still. He was a solid provider. We saw him on the weekends. I'm sure he played with us then and always gave us lots of love and affection, but we never knew what went on inside of him.

I begin the play *Family Secrets* with Mort, who is based on my father, for a couple of reasons. One is that his is the most elaborate costuming. In order to hide my ample bosom, I must pad

■ family secrets

my belly to meet the circumference of my breasts. He wears a three-piece suit, tie, shoes, a short black wig, and glasses. I have very little makeup on to help create the illusion that I am, in fact, a man. Once I appear on the stage I never leave. I transform from one character to the next, so the most difficult costume, and character, are shed and I can easily move into the less demanding costumes of the females.

Mort's monologue is an introduction to the other characters; he mentions them all. He is, in essence, the host of the evening. (And it's fun to hear people in the audience whisper, "I thought this was a one-*woman* show.")

My stage is simple yet elegant. Stage left there is a twin bed covered in dark blue velour. Center stage there is a forest green velour overstuffed chair. Next to it is a coffee table, with dramatic green plant (mother-in-law's tongue) and black telephone. Stage right there is a vanity, which holds all my wigs, glasses, and makeup and is the same red velour as the side table. It has a two-way mirror so I can see myself and the audience can see through the glass and watch my face transform into the next character. Flush stage right is the coat rack on which hang the rest of the costumes. Tucked behind the rack is a hamper where I will drop the costumes I have finished with. It is black, like the velour backdrop and carpet. The stage sparkles like a jewel box under the lights.

The preshow music fades, and up comes "In the Mood." I walk out as Mort now, in the dark. I go to the plush green chair and sit down. The house brims with people, still talking. I can see their shadows but they can't see me at all. I hear some shushing. I pick up the phone. I breathe, relax, stretch my leg. The music fades. I say my first line.

Uh-huh.
Uh-huh.
Uh-huh.

sherry glaser ▨

Yeah.

(Back lights come up.)

Uh-huh.

Uh-huh.

Fern? Fern? Can I ask you one question?

Why did you write the checks when the money wasn't there?

(Lights all the way up. Mort is on the phone. Thick black hair with distinguished dapples of gray, half glasses. Three-piece charcoal gray suit and black dress shoes. He loosens his tie.

Uh-huh.

(He scratches his chin and picks his nose. He examines his finding and flicks it into the air.)

Uh-huh.

All right, all right.

No, I'll talk to your mother about it and we'll call you back.

All right . . . all right.

Goodbye. *(He hangs up.)*

My oldest . . .

I tried to tell her not to buy a used Saab.

You know a few years ago she changed her name from Fern to Kahari.

I said, "What's Kahari?"

She said, "It's jungle blossom, Dad."

I said, "So, what's the matter with Fern?"

Then she decides she's not Jewish anymore.

I said, "What do you mean you're not Jewish?

I'm Jewish, your mother's Jewish, of course you're Jewish."

family secrets

She says, "No. I don't believe in God anymore. I worship the Goddess now and I'm a pagan witch."

So she's a witch.
I'm glad she's a witch, because that way, while her car is in the garage she can ride around on a broomstick.

Then she calls and she says, "Daddy, I'm in love."
I said, "Terrific."
I mean, it's not the first time.
She says, "No, I'm so excited. We're coming out to California for your anniversary so you can meet her."
"Her? Who her?"

She says, "You're gonna love her, Dad, her name is Molly and she's Jewish."
I said, "I don't care if she's a rabbi, I don't want to meet her."
She says, "Why not?"
I said, "Because it's not normal."
She says, "It's not normal to love someone?"
I said, "No . . . a woman."
She says, "You love Mom."
I said, "It's different."
She says, "Is it about sex?"
I said, "I don't want to talk about it."
She says, "Well, you enjoy having sex with a woman, why shouldn't I?"
I said, "I don't want to talk about it!" and I hung up.

(Rises from the chair.)

Now you gotta understand something . . .
For our twenty-fifth anniversary, Bev and I had decided we were going to renew our vows.
Everybody we know was gonna be there.

sherry glaser ▣

But Bev says, "Oh, but Mort, she's your daughter. Call her back. Tell her they can come. It will make her happy." I said, "Why is it my job to make her happy? I'm not calling her."
She says, "Fine, if it makes you happy don't call her."
I said, "It doesn't make me happy. It makes me miserable, but I'd rather be miserable than call her and make her happy."

(He goes over to clothing tree and starts to undress. He takes off his watch, empties his pockets, and takes off his jacket.)

Happy? Happy.
Where I come from happy was different.
Happy was simple.
I'm from the Bronx.
You gave me a stick and a ball, I was happy.
If my mother made spaghetti and she put a fried egg on top with some ketchup . . .
I was happy.
I went to school and became an accountant.
Got married, had kids, and we moved to Long Island, and every day for twenty years I took the Long Island Rail Road into the city on the six fifty-nine . . .
Why they never made it the seven, I don't know.
Came home on the five fifty-two, had dinner and a bowl of ice cream.
I fell asleep in front of the TV and I was happy.

(Picks up slippers and returns center stage.)

I told her, I said, "Bev, they're not coming, and that's final."
She says, "Okay, if they're not coming, I'm not coming."
You see how it works? That's how it works.

(He sits down muttering.)

family secrets

Okay, they can come.
They can come under one condition . . .
They can't touch.

So they fly out for the party and I meet Molly.
And she's a nice girl . . . for my son Joel . . . maybe.

(He rises.)

So, I'm talking to her and she says to me,
"Mr. Fisher, how do you feel about me and Kahari?"
I said, "You want to know the truth? I got a problem with
it."
She says, "Well, is it possible that it brings up your own
homosexual feelings?"

Anyway, the rabbi calls us over for the ceremony.
Would you believe I found the same rabbi who married
us in Brooklyn twenty-five years ago?
Yeah, he was retired, but we flew him out.

Beautiful ceremony. Beautiful.
Bev and I stood under the chupa, I broke the glass,
My mother sang "Sunrise, Sunset."
We're having a great time.

We saw friends and family, we saw some cousins we hadn't
seen in years.
After dinner we opened a bottle of scotch we got on our
wedding night.
My brother made a toast.
"To the Funny Valentines."
And then we had the band play our song, "My Funny
Valentine."
I take my wife out on the deck and we danced.
"Da da da da da, da da da da, da da daaaa da da da da."

And the bandleader says, "Everybody who's in love please join them."

I don't want to look, but I know. Everybody there is watching Molly dance with Kahari.

And I was ashamed. I was ashamed that she was my daughter and I couldn't talk to her for months and months and months, not after that.

(He turns and sits in chair.)

But eventually I had to call her because it was tax season and I'm her accountant.

So I called her up and I said, "Hello, this is your father. Are you going to send me your 1099s?"
She said, "No, I'm going to H & R Block this year."
That really hurt.
I said, "So that's it. We're not going to talk."
She said, "You're the one who stopped talking to me."
I said, "Well, you're the one who ruined my party and you humiliated me in front of everybody I know."
She says, "Well, I just want you to accept me for who I am."
I said, "Who the hell are you?"
She said, "I don't know, but I'm trying to find out what makes me happy."
I said, "Why can't you be happy like a normal person?"
She says, "What's normal?"
I said, "You find a nice guy. You have a house in the suburbs and a couple of kids. You settle down."
She says, "Do you think that would make me happy?"
I said, "I don't know, but it would make me happy."
She says, "Why is it my job to make you happy?"

I said, "It's not, and I want you to be happy. You're my daughter."

She says, "No matter what?"
I said, "Yeah, no matter what."
She says, "Good, because I'm gonna have a baby."

(He rises.)

Now I don't even want to consider the possibilities.
She says, "No, Daddy listen. Molly and I broke up. I met a
wonderful guy.
He's not Jewish."
I said, "That's all right."
She says, "His name is Miguel."
"Miguel?" I said. "Let me ask you something—are you
doing this to me on purpose?"
She said, "He loves me and wants the baby and I love
him."
I said, "All right . . . what does he do?"
"He's a trance channeler."
"I thought it was cable TV."
"No, Dad, he's a spiritual medium."
I said, "Is there any money in that?"
She said, "Don't worry, the universe will provide."

Would you like to see the universe?
*(He pulls his wallet out of his pocket and raises it over his head.
He starts to exit.)*

And I got two other kids besides her.

My youngest daughter, Sandra, she's sixteen and there's
nothing I can do about that.

*(He lays his wallet on the vanity and undresses while he speaks.
He takes off tie, followed by pants, then shirt, then underbelly.)*

My son? My son, Joel, graduated from Columbia University.
He got a degree in engineering.

sherry glaser

We were thrilled, so for a graduation present we send him over to Israel.

We don't hear from Joel for a couple of months.

Finally we get a postcard.

"Hi, Mom. Hi, Dad. I'm living on a kibbutz and I've become a shepherd."

I spend eighty-seven thousand dollars on his education.

He's on a hillside with a harmonica and some sheep.

Where did I get these kids?

I'll tell you one thing.

They take after their mother . . . and she's crazy.

My mother was a typical housewife. She stayed home, minded me, and, two and half years later, my brother Steven. In the afternoons she and her friends would gather at a neighbor's house, play mah jong, and drink whiskey sours. They shared recipes and hair-coloring tips, but they never spoke of their confusion, insecurities, or pain. They never discussed the destructive marriages they might have been a part of; they just gushed over those filled pastry horns or that fabulous home perm. While most women accepted and even excelled at their roles, at least cosmetically, my mother collapsed under its weight.

My mother wanted to be the perfect mother. Shelly Hassan had lost her mother when she was four. Her mother, Fanny, was crazy. Fanny had had to endure a long, complicated sanity trial, at which my mother had to testify about her mother's aberrant behavior. Shelly vowed that if she lived long enough and was fortunate enough to have her own children she would completely resolve and repair the damage done to her by becoming the perfect mother. But life got in the way. Steven and I didn't respond properly to Dr. Spock's elementary instructions. Then my mother read *Summerhill,* a book that detailed an alternative and more creative way of raising children. When my mother studied its pages, anticipating a great big pat on the back, she was rudely informed that she had been just the opposite of the consummate mother.

In comparison to the type of parent *Summerhill* celebrated, my mother appeared to be a tyrant, ruining our lives with her rigid rules and schedules. She didn't calculate in her love for us and her sincere effort. It was the small details (bedtime, creative development, chores) of child rearing that are so complicated where she fell short. She only saw her failure. Soon after President Kennedy was assassinated, my mother had a nervous breakdown. I was four years old, the same age as she was when she lost her mother.

Things had been a bit strange for a while. My mother would cry for no reason and sit staring at nothing for a long time. She would yell at me for leaving the top off the toothpaste; her outraged response was out of proportion to the infraction. Sometimes she would scream at me for no reason at all. She would let me sit on the roof of our new '64 red Chevy with my baby brother on my lap and slide down the windshield.

One afternoon we were sitting quietly on the cement porch steps. I was sitting very close to her. I loved to smell her Arpège and the Wrigley's spearmint gum she loved to chew. I would brush up against her smooth, cool skin. It was so soft and familiar. I was playing with a box full of costume jewelry given to me by various tias and old ladies from the neighborhood. They were in a terrible tangle. I turned to my mother and gave her the jumble of gold and silver necklaces and said, "Mommy, can you untangle these?" She didn't say a word. She lifted the mess from the box and started to cry. I got scared and covered my ears. She took the jewelry and threw it into the air and screamed and screamed. Beads and pearls bounced everywhere. Our neighbors, my mother's friends, Wanda and Lenore and all the kids in the neighborhood, Marshall and David, Kathy and the twins, started gathering. They stood in horror staring at my mother, whispering, with their hands cupped over their mouths. No one came forward to help me. The phone rang. I ran inside and answered it. It was my father. "Mommy's sick, Daddy. Come home." I stayed inside looking out the window occasionally while my mother ranted at the neighborhood. My baby brother started to cry from his crib, but I cried harder.

The ambulance came and two men corralled my mother and took her away. I suppose a neighbor stayed with me until my aunt arrived. It's hard to remember. I was a twisted web of guilt and terror. No one told me it wasn't my fault. No one explained anything to me. I was old enough to take responsibility for the whole incident, but I was too young to understand it. I remember the sound of my patent leather shoes marching down the marble floors of Hillside Hospital toward her room. I have no recollection of actually seeing her there. The rest of the time I was in some kind of void. My spirit left my body and went to protect her from the monsters that had finally come to get her. The whole nine months she was gone is a black hole in my memory.

When she had her nervous breakdown, my father disappeared. Well, to me he did. He was so busy with psychiatrists and pharmacists and continuing the nine to five, he couldn't take care of two little kids. So he moved into my Aunt Florrie's apartment while she and her husband, Uncle Paul, and their new baby, Melanie, moved into our house to take care of Steven and me. As far as I was concerned, I'd lost both Mommy and Daddy and found myself the child of new parents. I'm sure they loved me and tried to reassure me the best they could, but the impact of losing two parents was too much to bear. When I see pictures of myself at that time, I look like a depressed thirty-year-old, but I was only four.

family secrets

After mucho drugs—Stelazine, Thorazine, Compazine, a plethora of zines and twelve rounds of shock therapy my mother came back and so did my father. It was a miracle. We were one big, happy family again, but now there was the subtle threat that we were always on the brink of disaster. She could go at any time, and I made it my job to make sure she didn't.

Now I stand in Bev's silky black pants. My voice takes on the high, sharp tones of Bev. I take the blouse from the clothes tree and use the easy Velcro to fasten it and sing:

Crazy, I'm crazy for feeling so lonely.
Crazy, I'm crazy for feeling so blue.

I put on the scarf laid out on the vanity stool, followed by the wig and glasses and continue to sing.

I apply rouge and lipstick and brush my hair.

Brandi! Brandi!
Come on, Brandi.
Good boy. That's a good boy. *(She pets him emphatically.)*
No jumping, no. *(She holds his nose down.)*
Sit, sit.
Good boy.
Now, lay down. Lay down.

(She walks center stage and picks up her tea.)

I just got back from taking the dog to the chiropractor.
My husband thinks that's crazy, but Brandi gets so excited when we throw the ball for him that he runs into the wall and he gets out of alignment. *(Laughs)*

I know I spoil him, but he's my only baby.
My kids are grown-up.

My youngest daughter, Sandra, she's sixteen and there's nothing I can do for her.

But once you're a mother, you're always a mother.

(Laughs)

I wish someone had mothered me like that, but I lost my mother when I was four.

She went crazy.

They put her away and I never saw her again.

I swore to myself. I swore that I would be the perfect mother, and that's what drove me crazy. *(Laughs)*

Because that's impossible, right?

You'd have to have a perfect world.

And I tried to make perfect kids, but they wouldn't cooperate. *(Laughs)*

They got dirty. They fell down. They got sick.

And they were basically out to get me. *(Laughs)*

So in 1965 I had a nervous breakdown,

and you know something? It was the perfect time for me to go crazy.

My husband had a good job and we had major medical.

So I took advantage of it. *(Laughs)*

Not on purpose.

I tried. I tried with all my might not to go crazy, but one night I lost it.

I lost it because I was trying to make lasagna. *(Laughs)*

I went out and got all fresh ingredients.

Tomatoes, mushrooms, three different kinds of cheese and I spent three and a half hours in the kitchen and it turned out like hell. *(Laughs)*

I don't know, maybe the ricotta was bad. It doesn't matter.

The kids took one bite and they said,

"Mommy, this tastes horrible. We can't eat this."

And I said, "I spent three and a half hours in the kitchen.

family secrets

I don't care that it tastes like . . . you're gonna eat it."
(Laughs)

Well, nobody moved.
I said, "Okay, don't eat it. I'll just flush it down the toilet."
So I picked up the lasagna and the salad and the bread *(she does)* and I went into the bathroom
and I dumped the lasagna into the toilet, I put the salad on top and
I took the baguette and I'm pushing it down into the toilet. *(she does)*
And my husband is screaming at me. "Bev! The plumbing . . . the plumbing." *(Laughs)*

Now, here I am having a nervous breakdown and he's worried about the plumbing.
So I went after him with the baguette. *(She chases him, swatting the baguette.)*
Hitting him with this baguette . . . Lasagna is flying everywhere.
The kids are laughing and screaming and I guess somebody called the hospital because they came to get me.
And I was glad.
I mean, I really needed to get away. *(Laughs)*

So Mort came in the ambulance with me and he's saying to me,
"Bev, what is wrong with you?"
I said, "Why are you calling me Bev?"
He said, "That's your name."
I said, "My name is not Bev. My name is Mary."
He said, "Mary? Mary who?"
I said, "Mary, mother of Jesus."
Well, this upset him.
But I felt terrific.

Well, I was the perfect mother, right?

So I'm glad to get to the hospital, because I know there
are people there that really need me.
So Mort's got the forms, he's filling them out, and I go
around laying hands on everyone because I want to heal
them.
Nobody appreciated this, especially the one man who
thought he was Jesus.
But I knew he was crazy because my son was Jesus and he
was home.

But this doesn't stop me, because for the first time in years
I felt wonderful.
I went around that hospital singing *(she does)* and dancing
(she does) and having a wonderful time, until they sedated
me.

First they gave me Thorazine.
Then they gave me shock treatments.
Twelve shock treatments.
And I certainly felt no pain after that. I felt nothing.

So they kept us busy.
They taught us ballroom dancing. They taught us fencing.
They taught us how to play bridge.
But you know what they did?
They gave us bridge lessons on Monday and shock treat-
ment on Tuesday,
so by Wednesday, none of us could play a hand. *(Laughs)*

So this went on for six months and then it was their procedure to let you go.
They had no idea what was wrong with me,
so they put me on Compazine and sent me home.

⬛ family secrets

You know what Compazine is? It's mild Thorazine.
So after all that, I'm depressed and I stayed depressed till
we moved to California, ten years later.

But when we came here to California, that's when I
found my therapist, Bunny.
She's terrific.
She's the one who finally diagnosed me as manic depressive.
That means that I have highs, incredible highs, and lows
because I have a chemical imbalance in my brain.
What they prescribe for that is lithium.
It's a salt, comes from the ground, so now I'm grounded.
(Laughs)
And when I leveled off she said, "Okay, now let's get to
the source of your problem.
You're afraid. You're afraid of your feelings, so you repress
your feelings.
Let's start with the hard one. Anger.
Who are you mad at?"
"I'm not mad at anyone."
"Oh no?"

She took me into her basement where she had cartons full
of plates.
She handed me a plate and said, "Take this, smash it on
the floor and say, 'I hate my children.'
I said, "I could never say that."
She said, "Try it." *(Takes the plate and raises it above her head
and smashes it.)*
I hate my children . . . Let me have another one. *(Laughs)*

The kids took about eight or nine plates.
My husband was ten or twelve, and would you believe we
ran out of plates on my mother?

sherry glaser ◪

I said, "I'm still mad at her."
She said, "You *should* be angry. You were abandoned."
I said, "I know that. I thought it was my fault."
She said, "It had nothing to do with you. It was your
mother's thing. Now you've got to express your anger and
get on with your life."
"How? How do I do that?"
She said, "Confront her."
I said, "She's dead."
"Then go to her grave."
"She was cremated and her ashes are with my brother in
New York."
She said, "Well, let's get her out here."

So what am I gonna do?
I call my brother and I say, "Listen, Lenny, I really need to
see Mama, could you please send her out."
Well, he was reluctant at first.
He said, "I'm afraid she'll get lost in the mail."
I said, "Okay, let's send her Federal Express, she'll be fine."

And you know, when I saw that Federal Express truck
come down my driveway I was ready to let her have it.
I took the package. *(She does.)*
And I brought her into my living room. *(She sits with pack-
age on her lap.)*
I opened the box and there was an urn, so I opened it.
And I stuck my hands into the ashes.
And it wasn't really ash, it's more like gravel and little
pieces of her bones.
And it hit me . . . the grief.

For the little girl. *(Laughs)*
For the little girl inside me that had to grow up all alone.
And for her . . . for her.

family secrets

For the poor woman, who was so lost out there she
couldn't even get to know her own daughter.
And the only way I could get to know my mother was to
go crazy.

And I realized something.
I realized that through all this time and the craziness and
even through death that she was my mother.
And I let her go . . . I let her go.

And I looked down and my mother was all over the place.
So I cleaned her up as best I could. *(She does.)*
but I felt very funny the next time I had to vacuum in
here.
But what a healing. *(She rises.)*
What a healing.
And of course I still take one day at a time.
I'm still on lithium, so I'm not perfect, but I'm here.
I raised my kids and they are terrific.
My daughter Fern is an artist.
My son Joel is in Israel, and Sandra . . . we'll see. *(Laughs)*

And I'm in law school. *(Starts exit to vanity.)*
I'm gonna be a judge. *(Laughs)*

(At vanity takes off scarf and tosses into hamper; pants follow.)

And I'm very proud of myself and you know something?
I think my mother is too.
Because once you're a mother, you're always a mother.
Right? *(Laughs and takes off wig, glasses, and blouse with one
motion.)*

   I was a sickly child. I went to the doctor frequently. Not just
for the usual checkups and booster shots. I had gastroenteritis by
the time I was eight. I had constant strep throat and earaches. I

liked being sick. I got lots of attention and I didn't have to go to school. I could stay home and watch my mother. The great thing was nobody noticed this connection, they just thought I had a weak constitution.

Every time I didn't want to go to school (which was quite often) I would say I had a sore throat. No one doubted me. I was so good at it I could actually manifest those nasty bacteria. I was so skilled an invalid I managed to get my tonsils removed because of repeated infections. Of course, I wasn't conscious of what I was doing at the time. But I can see now the twofold terror I faced. One was the possibility that if I left my mother alone, she would end up back in the hospital by the end of the day. The other fear was of school itself. All those strangers! Sure, they were my height, but I didn't know what to say to them. What I really needed was a psychiatrist, but who knew? Everyone just assumed I was shy. I was always very well behaved. I wouldn't do anything to upset anybody because the last time I had upset someone, they took her away to a mental hospital. I couldn't express myself. The throat, a symbol of expression, trapped all the fear for me and manifested itself as illness.

The gastroenteritis was in my stomach, the center of emotional issues. I was so worried all the time about my mother and her illness that I was an eight-year-old on the verge of an ulcer.

We moved to Howard Beach, in Queens, to what we thought was a posh apartment complex called Pembroke Square on Linden Boulevard. My aunt and uncle lived in the next building. My mother and her sister chose to live within minutes of each other partly because they had been separated throughout their childhood.

My grandmother, because of her insanity, and grandfather, because of brain damage, weren't really fit to care for their children. Florrie was frail and subject to many illnesses, so she was fortunate to be taken in by her grandparents. My mother endured crazy parents and a series of treacherous foster homes.

　　　　　　　　　　　　　　　　　　　　　⊠ family secrets

When Florrie and Shelly grew up, it was as if they had made a pact never to be apart again. There was also the convenience of having family and the cousins close in case something happened to my mother again.

We lived in Lobby L. We got a dog. We went to the Bide-A-Wee home and Steven and I were allowed to pick any dog we wanted. We walked down the long metal corridor staring into the begging eyes of these poor, abandoned creatures. It was almost too much for me to bear. I knew the fate that awaited them. How could I play accomplice to that kind of murder? How could I leave there without all of them? Happy was a white mutt with tawny markings. He was lying down so quietly, just staring up at us. He looked completely bereft. They said he was a husky mix and the reason his previous family had given him up was because he showed his teeth too often. We later discovered it was the way Happy smiled. I loved this dog. He was my trusted companion and confidant. He knew everything about me and he loved me no matter what I did.

The problem was that Happy would run away. If the apartment door was left open for a split second, Happy would be out the door; if the doors to the apartment complex were open he would jet through those as well. Our building was very close to the highway. I would shake with terror and scream, "God damn it, Happy!" as I gave chase, but I always had to stop at the curb. My father would tear out after the fugitive and I would run back to the apartment and keep a prayer vigil until Happy was carried back in my father's arms. My father hated Happy and cursed him all the time.

My mother was mostly on an even keel at this point, but she'd get particularly aggravated if we were having company. I thought having company was fun and holidays were festive, but with the relatives came her most manic periods. She would be in a frenzy of cleaning, and if we all weren't cooperating, vacuuming, dusting, and putting hospital corners on all the beds, she would get really quiet. There would be this evil snarl on her face that sent me scurrying under my bed protected by the dangling white cotton balls that hung from the hem of my bedspread. But when the guests arrived, she was vivacious and bubbly, the belle of the ball.

One night, my mother was getting ready to go out for a fancy evening with my father. She had her hair in curlers and she was wearing her black slip and bra. At the time she fixed her mascara to look like sweeping batwings. She looked like she had escaped from Transylvania. She called for my brother to do something and there was no answer. She scoured the apartment, but she couldn't find Steven. She said, "When I find him I'm gonna kill him," and she picked up a pair of scissors and went searching for him. I found Steven in his toy box. I told him to stay there until I calmed my mother down. I don't think she would have really cut my brother to shreds, but at that point I really didn't have any guarantees.

It wasn't long before my mother became the leader of my Brownie troop, where we sewed "sit upons" and made authentic Pakistani food. Everyone thought my mother was the most entertaining and creative mother around. Brownies gave me something wholesome and reliable for a while and I worked hard at upholding the Girl Scout law and keeping my uniform neatly ironed and tidy. I envisioned my mother and me getting the Junior and Brownie Leader Award of the Year. The ceremony would be complete with parading Brownies and Girl Scouts all in single file with votive candles, singing our theme song, "Kumbiya."

One afternoon, when I was seven, I was playing by myself in the playground outside our apartment building in Howard Beach. It was a gray, cold day. I knew I had to go in soon, but I loved to swing and play on the monkey bars by myself. I could

✶ family secrets

try out new routines and not feel awkward as I often did in front of the always more agile children. A man came up to me and asked me if I knew where the bathroom was. Now of course, my mother had told me never to talk to strangers, but he needed to go to the bathroom and it would have been cruel of me to ignore him. I said, "It's there, around the building, in the back."

"Would you show me?" I couldn't say no at this point. It would have been rude.

I brought him around to the back and showed him the door. He took my hand and pulled me in with him. I was frozen in terror. The stench of the bathroom and his stale, toxic breath suffocated me. He took down his pants and flapped his penis in my face and told me to touch it. I wouldn't. I couldn't. But he took my hand and made me stroke it. It was soft and rubbery, but it was full of danger. He dropped my hand to remove his pants entirely, and I bolted. I ran out the door crying and running as fast as I could to Lobby L. I didn't tell my mother. I was sure she would be angry with me because I had talked to a stranger and it really was my fault. Instead I took Happy into my room and told him. It was our secret.

My mother suspected something was wrong. I was either extremely emotional or I had my "Sherry face" on. My "Sherry face" was blank of all expression; it was like a death mask. It frightened and offended my mother. I finally told her about the incident. She was crying and couldn't let me finish. She asked me why I took the man to the bathroom when she had warned me against talking to strangers and especially going anywhere with them. I told her I was just trying to be a good Brownie. So I got my "Taking the dirty old man to the bathroom" merit badge.

We moved to Long Island because my parents were afraid of sending me to public school in Howard Beach. There had been a story circulating that at P.S. 232 a girl had had her pigtails cut off by a boy who had brought a pocketknife to school with him. So we moved.

Oceanside was "safe." It was a new community built on a landfill. Poorly built. I can still see my father in his nightly routine. He would relax on the autumn gold shag carpet in the family room and alternate between watching TV and dozing off. Suddenly one of his arms would shoot up toward the ceiling. "I feel a draft!" He would try to trace the draft to its source, his arms frantically searching around and above his head, "Where's that goddamn draft coming from?" It drove him insane. Years later, when we were replacing the window seat in the kitchen, we found old beer bottles thrown in there; it had been insulated with cardboard.

We lived in a Jewish neighborhood. There was only one set of Christmas lights up in December; they belonged to the Lodicos on Sally Lane. Everyone else had a menorah. The only black person in my school was the custodian. I was living in a vacuum and I thought the whole world was like that. All men were accountants, brokers, attorneys, garment center salesmen or Wall Street types. Some of the women had part-time jobs as secretaries or dental assistants, a few were getting into real estate, but most of the women stayed home and took care of the kids and the house. They were only two kinds of houses, a Splanch (a split-level ranch style) and a Colonial. We lived in a Colonial.

My room was painted hot pink, even the ceiling. The carpet was red. It was ripe for rage. The fuchsia walls were covered with adorable animal posters, lions, and their cubs, leopards frolicking, pandas munching bamboo. My red wooden shelves boasted a doll collection from all over the world. I had a huge stuffed animal collection. I slept with those animals often and couldn't just sleep with one, because I was sure the others would feel bad. I had to pile them all on my bed and I slept scrunched up at the top. The bureau was white, as were the bookshelves. The room was a visual assault.

　　　　　　　　　　　　　　📖　family secrets

My brother's room was adjacent to mine. It was a study in olive green and brown, accented with a cowboy-and-Indian bedspread. Steven stayed in his room and I stayed in mine. I thought he was retarded. He could sit in front of the TV for hours and drool. He loved cartoons and science fiction and at night sometimes he would stare into space and claim he was trying to move a glass of water across the room, over on his desk, with just the power of his mind. We got along better after he let me get him high.

My parents' bedroom was down the hallway on the other side of the house. It was a tribute to gold, as was the rest of the house. All the carpet downstairs was gold. The couch was gold, the refrigerator and all the appliances were gold. It was the Royal Colonial.

We had a '64 red Chevy, a '72 blue LeSabre in the garage and perfectly arranged grassy green sod covering our modest plot of suburban security: 98 Jeffery Lane.

Moving to Long Island was my father's goal. To have our own house, and backyard, a place for Happy to run around. He left the house while it was still dark. He drove the old Chevy to the Oceanside train station and got on the six fifty-nine. He was usually at the office at eight o'clock. He worked for Harry Winston for a while and would bring home brochures of all the beautiful diamonds and emeralds and rubies. They provided him with box seats for Yankee games. He was at the game where Roger Maris hit his sixty-ninth home run. He still has the scorecard.

By the time we got to Long Island he worked at Chem Systems in Manhattan as chief executive comptroller. On occasion I went to work with him. I'd usually go in during Christmas break from school. I loved going on the train with Daddy, still sleepy-eyed and cold from the rude awakening at seven o'clock (He'd take the later train to accommodate me). Coming off the railroad, there were so many people, all moving so quickly, that someone as small as myself might merely lift my feet from the ground and be carried along to my destination. When we emerged from the station, everyone's black umbrellas would shoot open in synchronized wonder.

My father would even pay me for my day's assistance. I could file. I was very good at it and there was always so much to be done. It was at this place I dreamed of becoming a secretary, just like Rose Barbera, his faithful companion for the eight years he was there.

When my father walked down the corridor of his office everyone said "Hello." I was sure, because of the way he carried himself and everyone's high respect for him, that he really was the president of the company. I loved those days with him. I felt so close to him, so lucky.

But most days he went off all by himself for twelve to thirteen hours. When he came home we would have dinner every night at seven o'clock. Lucy was on TV; so was *Star Trek*. My brother loved *Star Trek*. I loved Lucy. We had to alternate. Sometimes my father would insist on having the news on. But the TV always accompanied our repast. We sometimes watched it, but we always talked over it as well. It was just as much a part of the family as our dog.

After dinner, Steven and I would clear the dishes and my mother would sit on my father's lap and they would kiss. I thought this was sick; so did Steven. We couldn't believe our parents could engage in such disgusting behavior. We would retch and complain throughout, but I would try to catch a real glimpse of the kiss if I could. They ignored us. They were in love.

They had their fights too. One of my major preoccupations (besides death and the thought of my parents being locked in a movie theater or restaurant and me being stuck with a baby sitter the rest of my life) was my parents getting a divorce.

family secrets

They fought freely and unabashedly and they made up with the same gusto. I'm proud to say I take after them in this way. There is a love between them that accepts all the blemishes and warts and the annoying habits and the sometimes devastating rituals of the other. I think it is an unconditional and inspiring kind of love. After the dishes there would be more TV. My father would usually be set up on a tray table and do work, either for his company or for private tax clients. Sometimes he would lie on the floor and watch TV and call for a blanket. He would thank the giver with a kiss or a hug or a rub. He loved us.

He made lots of money and we always had everything we needed and wanted. But who he really was, was the mystery. He called me last year and apologized for that, saying he had missed our childhood and that he was sorry, it's something you just can't buy back.

I met Heidi Askenazy in Mrs. Sodemann's fourth-grade class. She lived on Greentree Drive in a Splanch. We were friends at school, but a block and a half was far away to my mother so we didn't see each other much after school, at first.

Our next door neighbors were the Mars. Kelly and Jack and their kids, Dara and Stuie. For some reason, Stuie hated my brother and made his life a living hell until my brother learned karate and gave Stuie a chop in the nose. Dara was my enemy.

We started out as friends. We played nicely and we played dirty. A couple of times we ended up in the closet. Me with a battery in my panties as a penis substitute and Dara, half naked, rubbing our anxious smooth skin together. But when we went to Treasure Island summer camp together, Dara became involved with the popular girls. For some reason they really didn't like me and excluded me from the sacred hairbrushing and nail-painting rituals. That kind of exclusion sent me into a frenzy of trying to win these girls over. I would smile and always say hello and try to think of something to start a conversation, or bring

sherry glaser

something to camp that I loved, and even give it to one of them. I had only one friend. Her name was Jody. I think it happened that way because Jody and I were fat. We were nice people, but we were fat. Dara was tiny, like a bird.

I asked my mother, "Am I fat?" "No," she said, "You're zaftig." (Which means fat in Yiddish.) It was the kind of fat that you are before you get breasts. Someday all that pudge around my waist would rise into my chest, but until then it was agony. My mother was always on a diet. One of her most notorious endeavors was "Think Thin." The secret to the success of this diet was that everything was cooked in one pot and the result was so tasteless that you usually wouldn't eat much. She had a huge magnet on the refrigerator of an apple with a belt cinched tight around its belly. "Think Thin" it shouted. I tried to diet too, but I loved food too much. It was the only comfort I understood.

Heidi and I weren't in the same class in fifth grade. We reunited in sixth grade in Mrs. Pollack's class. That's also where we met Fred and Steve and Kevin and where boys became a permanent source of angst in my life. Heidi and I talked so much in class that we had to be separated constantly. Heidi was louder and would sass back to Mrs. Pollack. Heidi got detention. A lot. We made up a song about it. I would wait for Heidi in the playground and when she was liberated we would stay for another hour and play and sing. I did a great imitation of Barbra Streisand and I would belt out "People" and hurl myself around the pole that held up the swings. We laughed so hard we'd pee in our pants. Every time Heidi and I were together we'd pee. It was great.

There was a huge garbage dump in Oceanside. Since Oceanside is terminally flat this was our mountain. Heidi and I were very concerned about the amount of garbage, so we decided to confront the sanitation department. We wrote an environmental song to the tune of "With a Little Help from My Friends" and went over on our bicycles and sang for the garbage executives.

▓ family secrets

The gents applauded politely, but when I left Oceanside five years later the mountain was an Everest.

Heidi wasn't skinny. She came from a long line of belly dancers and was full of Sephardic curves, which made me very happy and comfortable around her. She was adorable. She was short and bouncy and had dark hair and eyes with a devilish spark. Her laugh was deep and warm and gurgly like a Jacuzzi. And Freddie liked her. Nobody liked me. Oh, they liked me as a friend and all. I made sure of that. Every day I would bring a box of Bazooka gum to school with me and I would supply all the kids I wanted for friends, but nobody wanted me as a girl-friend. I was fat and I was sure, with new explosions on my face everyday (which I faithfully squoze), that I was ugly.

I hated myself. I would slash and pinch my face while looking in the mirror. I would slam my wrist, forearm, calf, or ankle against the doorframe, not only to feel the pain, but hoping to end up with a broken bone. I wanted a cast so badly. I thought everybody would want to sign it and, well, maybe one of the boys would fall in love with me during a particularly poetic signing. I did get myself on crutches for a while and I was fairly content. My pain threshold hardly existed.

I liked Kevin. He was an Irish angel. He looked like John Boy from *The Waltons*. I wrote him anonymous letters (never sent) and gave him extra gum. He liked Laura, who was cute and blond and a size one. It didn't help me that a new friend of mine in Mr. Shlissel's biology class called me "Ugly" as a nickname. I'm not sure if I was ugly. My nose and chin were prominent and I was always pale. When I see pictures of myself, I think I was plain. Plain, and very insecure.

When I was thirteen I developed ovarian cysts. This got me to new and exciting doctors, gynecologists. I was in way over my head. These guys liked to perform surgery and could remove crucial parts of my anatomy. Dr. B was suspicious that these little fibrous jewels were cancer. He wanted me to go in for exploratory surgery. They would go in through the vagina, no incision, and take a look around. I was in the hospital, on my thirteenth birthday. I got mounds of attention, the stuff I had been yearning for, but I was scared too. I was in the pediatrics wing. I shared the room with another girl. She was having a lump removed from her spine. The night before surgery we got our sleeping pills and we talked. She said, "Are you Jewish?" I said, "Yes. Why?"

"If you die in surgery tomorrow, you'll go straight to hell. Good night."

I pulled through. But the cyst Dr. B spied through his magic wandering instrument was the size of a grapefruit. Dr. B was 90 percent sure it was cancer and wanted to remove the offending ovary, maybe both. My mother said, "No. We're going to get a second opinion." So we did. We got a second that concurred with Dr. B's. The third opinion, from Dr. Stephen Goldman, a chiropractor, was my salvation. He could feel the cyst and said he could tell by my pulse that I was way out of balance. He recommended I soak my lower abdomen with cloths dipped in castor oil, covered by a heating pad, for one hour a day. He would adjust me weekly. We agreed to the treatment and the cysts went away and never came back.

I believe the mystery of the cysts had to do with my creativity. I was born with a creative spark. Before the collapse of my psyche and my family, I was a born actress, singer, dancer, poet. I would create all sorts of dramas alone in my room and I knew all the nursery rhymes and sang them with feeling. I wrote my first haiku in first grade. But my mother's disappearance and my assumption of responsibility for that drove my creative nature into the shadows. Being creative put me in too vulnerable a position.

family secrets

My nature was to create, but adolescence and hormones combined with the insecurity I had nurtured so long was an iron curtain to the Muses. Instead of creating poetry and drama, I created disease. Lucky for me I had found a way to survive. The constant realignment of my body, at the chiropractor, gave me a message that I wanted to live, that I had the power to heal and I had a tremendous will. A will so strong that I could overcome anything. Even being a teenager.

There was another benefit to my illness. I lost weight. I was really skinny from being on intravenous for a week or so. I loved the tight skin around my belly and the lack of cushion in my seat, but I knew it would come back in time. Food called to me like a lover.

Heidi and I spent every afternoon together, until she got a spot on the cheerleading squad. I was going to try out too, but I couldn't really do a split. I've never really been very bouncy, and the idea of being judged by all those perky, perfect gymnasts made me shudder. And Fred wanted her time. Heidi usually included me in plans with Fred. We'd hang out with Andy and Tommy and Albert. I was just one of the guys. We'd hang out at the Plaza, smoke pot, laugh.

Heidi and I would do our homework together. At least we *said* we were doing our homework. She would end up eating over almost every night and on weekends she'd sleep over. That's how we came up with two games. The first was the feather tickle. We both loved to be tickled on our backs, so we would take off our pajamas and take turns doing it to each other. The fun part was when we would "turn over" and tickle down the arms and belly and legs and come over so close to our freshly budded breasts. We'd tease each other for hours. It was sensual bliss.

The other game was more dangerous. Heidi initiated it. We'd ride our bikes to Oceanside Diner and order tuna salad and

Russian dressing and lots of challah. We'd get French fries and Coke and usually some sort of cookie for dessert if we could afford it. Sometimes after that, we'd go and have pizza too. After riding home, we'd get into ice cream and Entenmann's chocolate-chip cookies and eat until we were ready to explode. Then we'd go into the bathroom and take turns throwing up. The game was to see who could get the most out. I could eat whatever I wanted and not worry about being fat anymore. Heidi played the game only with me. I played it all the time.

I spent the next ten years of my life strategizing where I could get rid of my next meal. It was easy at home. After school I'd watch the four-thirty movie on TV and eat, usually half a loaf of white bread and vinegar or mustard sandwiches, and ice cream or cookies. I'd go upstairs to my bathroom, run the water a bit and rid myself of the afternoon snack. Restaurants were more difficult, especially if there were stalls. I'd have to sit so my feet were facing forward and throw up between my legs, silently. It was hard on my back, but nothing would stop me. Nobody ever found out. I was smart about it. I'd eat all the crappy food I wanted and vomit, but then I'd make sure I'd have salad and some sort of protein, and vegetables. It was such a position of power. At least that's how I felt when I was purging. I was in control. I had been in pain for a long time, but I couldn't control it. By self-destructing, I knew where the pain was coming from. It was a relief.

My introduction to sex came when I was fourteen, from Heidi's boyfriend, Fred. It was a secret. Heidi had been clear with him: She wasn't ready to have sex. I, however, was desperate for attention. I wanted him to want me. I wanted someone to want me. One day I was helping him with his homework at his house, as I did quite often. I was smart and I was always a good student. We went into the basement rumpus room to work. He mixed us screwdrivers (basically vodka with a dash of orange juice) and he rolled up a joint. After about five minutes

family secrets

of this I was really quite out of it, but loving the hormonal explosion. I actually felt kind of attractive when I was high. He asked me if I ever gave a blow job. I said, "No." He said he would show me how.

I wouldn't say he showed me. I'd say he forced me. He held my head and used me and gagged me until he was done with me. He said, "Wow, Sheryl! You're the best!" and because of the proclamation I was his to use, at his leisure and convenience. He never kissed me or had intercourse with me, or hugged me or said I was pretty or nice. I was betraying my best friend, so I could be treated like a hole. At this point I was throwing up two to three times a day. So I was an empty hole.

I was completely defined by what was going on outside of me. I was terrified and worried all the time. All I could do was numb myself with drugs and alcohol and cigarettes. It was during this time that Freddie stole a school bus and was busted by the cops and ended up going to reform school. We were all sad to see him go. Somehow I thought it was my fault or that I could have prevented it.

In high school I had a little more confidence; because of the drugs and because of the common fury of teenagers, I had more friends. Sure, we all used drugs, but we had each other. We were all lost together. We'd cut class and go out to the front of the school and get high. We did this every day. I sold joints. I'd buy a quarter pound of pot and use my mother's flour sifter to get all the seeds out. A dollar a joint. We'd trip out on Pink Floyd's *Dark Side of the Moon*.

There was a party every weekend. I usually told my parents I was sleeping at a friend's house. They actually trusted me and never checked up on me. One night there was a party where the parents were going to be in the house, so there could be no drinking or smoking at the party; we'd have to do the damage before we got there. A couple of friends and I got a fifth of Southern Comfort and we guzzled it before we got to the party.

We trudged off to the party, not feeling much and being disappointed that we'd have to attend the festivities quite sober. Somewhere around nine o'clock somebody pulled the shades down over my eyes. My friends told me what happened after that.

I became delirious. I threw up in the living room and some kids helped me into the bathroom. Everyone was afraid the adults would see how sick I was and they wanted to get me out of the house and into the cool air. Gary and Dave tried to revive me by sticking my head in the snow, but I was dead drunk and so heavy that they dropped me and I hit my head on the sewer. Finally, someone thought it would be a good idea to call my parents.

My mother came to get me. Gary and Steve dragged me into the car and held me up while my mother drove me home. I was asking Gary for Quaaludes on the way. Luckily, my mother had no pharmacological vocabulary, and Gary said I was just talking nonsense.

When I woke up in the morning my mother was asleep in a chair next to my bed. I was in my own bed and wearing pajamas, and I had no idea how I had gotten there. I groaned. My mother opened her eyes.

"Do you know where you are?"

"Yes."

"Do you know your name?"

"Yes."

"What is it?"

"Oh, Mom."

"What is it?" She was *pissed*.

"Sheryl Glaser."

"Where do you live?" I tried not to laugh out loud.

"Ninety-eight Jeffery Lane, Oceanside, Long Island 11572."

"Your father wants to see you." We walked into my parents' bedroom and my father looked horrendous. It looked like he had been up all night crying. He said, "Do you know what happened last night?"

"No, not really."

"What did you take?"

"I don't know. Someone handed me something in a glass. I didn't ask what it was and I drank it."

"Are you an alcoholic?"

"No." I was insulted. I took a lot more drugs than alcohol. "No. I told you I don't know what happened. I didn't do it on purpose. How do you think I feel?" I wasn't allowed out that night. I was glad, because my body was really fucked up anyway, but when I heard the story I was humiliated. I wasn't concerned that I had nearly died in a drunken stupor. I was more concerned that I looked foolish and disgusting throwing up, ugly drunk, in front of my friends. How could I ever be seen again?

Fred was out of reform school now and sort of back with Heidi. I was in love with David. He was in my home room. I could barely talk to him. I'd spend hours writing down possible topics of conversation. Well, he didn't talk much anyway, but he looked liked Neil Young to me.

The only problem was, he had a girlfriend. She was about four feet nine and had long straight brown hair and perfect skin. I thought she had an annoying voice, but he liked her. Okay, he loved her. But David and I were friends. We'd hang out in his neighborhood with the guys. He and I never really talked. I was much better friends with everyone else. It was his unavailability that drove me wild. I was determined that I would give him my virginity, like a Hanukkah present.

My best friend at the time was Merry. Of course they called us Shmerry. I hated that. We had met in Mr. Savage's Spanish class and our common ground was our interest in boys. We would go out together with the express determination of finding a boy to make out with. It was perfectly acceptable to leave the other one stranded if one trapped a male of the species. Merry's parents

sherry glaser ▨

were going away for the weekend and we planned a blowout party. We would get Quaaludes and invite David and Peter. We would split the Quaaludes with them and then give them the ultimate prize, our hymens.

David was playing pool when I approached him and asked if he'd like to share the Quaalude. He smiled. We ate it. Quaaludes were the aphrodisiac of choice. It was a downer that slowed everything down and melted all boundaries; you could be one with someone's whisper. About half an hour later David and I were in Merry's bedroom. There were no words, but words aren't what Quaaludes inspire. Kissing him was heavenly. He was gentle and very sensual. I got to touch his beautiful long brown hair. Even though we were blitzed on this horse tranquilizer, I felt he cared about me. I knew he did when he actually went down on me. I wasn't sure what was happening at first, but it became perfectly clear in a moment. I was scared and overwhelmed; nothing had ever felt so good in my life. I felt he loved me. Why else would he do something so intimate? Then he got inside me and kissed me the whole time. I was so happy. Goodbye, Virginity. There was hope. He left sometime in the night.

For some reason I thought he would be mine after that. But he was hers. He didn't call the next day, not that he said that he would, but . . . and on Monday he was back out in front of school with the skinny one. Our exchange was a secret. My whole life was silent. I was smothering in secrets. We had sex with each other a couple more times—once under the boardwalk in Long Beach, (very uncomfortable and sandy) and once in his bedroom while his parents were away. I longed for him all the time and seeing him with her ruined every day. I threw up a lot.

David and I ended up in Amy's office. Amy was the school psychologist. She might have saved my life. David needed to stop seeing me and be up front with his girlfriend. Amy helped him confront me and tell me the truth. He said he loved me and

family secrets

wrote me a poem and said it was over. I kept that poem with me all the time and started seeing Amy once a week. I don't remember anything I learned in school that year, but I remember finally having someone to talk to. Amy helped me realize that I wasn't worthless, that I would find a boyfriend and even if I didn't right away, I had a lot of friends. She suggested I stop taking drugs (which I didn't) and she never knew about the bulimia. But she knew something about me, about the beginnings of my pain. I began to articulate some of the anguish I felt.

About a month later I met Eddie. He was sweet and cute and a year older than I was. He could drive. He was my first boyfriend, and everyone knew it. He told me I was pretty.

We went out to concerts and movies and took a lot of drugs and drank. We were having fun. It was inspiring to be loved. He drove a black Caddy and I sat next to him in the front seat. We had sex all the time, but I never got pregnant. I was very lucky. One afternoon after a snack of milk and cookies we were fucking in his parents' bedroom and his mother came home. She was furious and pretty disappointed in us both. I was mortified. I had presented this demure image to her, the polite, good little girl, perfect for her son, and here I was soiling her precious sheets with my essential fluids. It was hard to face her after that, but my relationship with Eddie ended on a much more tragic note.

Eddie was delivering pizzas for a restaurant in Rockville Center. Merry and I would hang out there every afternoon and eat and get high with the Palmieri brothers. One rainy night Eddie was delivering pizzas and could barely see out the windshield. A boy on a bicycle darted out from around a corner and Eddie hit him and the boy died. I was too young and too selfish to help Eddie deal with his tragedy. He withdrew and we broke up. I met Eddie years later out in California. He looked gorgeous, still had his boyish grin and youthful, hard body. He had become an accountant. My father would have been thrilled had we ended up at the altar.

sherry glaser ▪

The character of Sandra is the kind keeper of this still tender teen biography. It is a relief to have a vessel to sail my pain away in, because even now I carry the penetrating scars of adolescence.

And I'm sick of it.
Every day in this house it's the same thing. *(Sandra throws on an oversized T-shirt and messes up her hair as she speaks.)*
Sandra, did you do this? Sandra, did you do that?
Sandra, Sandra, Sandra!
If I could get one minute of peace and quiet in this house that would be a miracle.
A miracle.

(Loud rock and roll. She finishes at the mirror and leaps on stage dancing hard.)

(Stops dancing and listens)
(Shouts)
What??????
What??????????

(She reluctantly turns off stereo.)

What!
Chicken? I hate chicken.
How long have you known me?
Well, have I ever liked chicken?
Oh . . . Kentucky Fried chicken . . . Okay.

My mother, she's driving me crazy.
It's just that her voice is so annoying.
We are having the biggest fight because . . .
Okay . . . It's my job to load the dishwasher, but she wants me to wash the dishes before I load them.
So I said to her, "Why? Why do I have to wash the dishes if it's a dishwasher?"

▨ family secrets

And she goes, "Because *(in mocking voice)* it's my dishwasher and it's my house.
And when you have your own dishwasher and your own
house . . . "
*(She sticks her fingers down her throat and falls back on the bed
and off it.)*

She's so pissed off at me. I can't believe it.
She found my pot.
I left this joint in the fireplace cause I was blowing the
smoke up the chimney.
And get this . . . get this.
She goes *(she rises)*, "Sandra, this is a cry for help.
Now I want you to tell me who your pusher is."
I said, "Okay, It's Mr. Zimberg, our principal."
She freaked, she freaked out. She grounded me and she
took away my allowance.
So now I have to start dealing.

She does this all the time.
Just when my life is going really really good, she tries to
ruin it.
Because last night was the most beautiful night of my life.

See, my parents went to this bar mitzvah.
So me and Heidi Askenazy had this huge party.
We got a case of Southern Comfort, a keg of beer.
We got really high.
It was just nice to be around normal people.

About ten o'clock in walks
Paul Levine, Richie Cohen, and . . . Stevie Fine.
Stevie Fine . . . I have had a crush on Stevie Fine forever.
We're in the same home room.
Fine, Fisher.

But he never noticed me until Friday.
We had a chemistry test and I let him cheat off me.
He comes up to me after class and he whispered in my
ear,
"Sandra, you saved my life."

So I invited him to this party, but I didn't think he would
come because, well . . .
he kind of has a girlfriend.
Stacie Klingler.
She thinks she is such hot shit, because she is the president
of Key Club.
Key Club. What is that?

(She acts out.)
Oh, I'll get the door, No, I'll get the door . . .
Well, I've got the key. *(She falls into the chair.)*

And she is so skinny, I hate her.
But when she finds out what happened last night, she's
gonna die.
Stevie said he would call me tonight.
(Lowers her head to the phone.)
Please call me . . . please.
I was thinking we could go out tonight, but now . . .
I'm under house arrest *(she screams "arrest")*
because they don't know what else to do with me.

You know they do?
They treat me like their slave.
You know I do everything in this house?
My mother does nothing.
All she does is go to work, come home, and cook dinner.
That's it.

Oh, now she goes to law school, big deal.

I go to school too, but I am the one who has to vacuum
this entire house and there's carpeting everywhere and she
wants all the lines to go one way.
(She lowers her head to phone again.)

Do you think I should call Stevie?
Do you think I should?
Ok, I'm going to call him, but if he answers, I'm just go-
ing to hang up.
(She picks up phone to dial, hears a voice, puts phone to her ear.)

Mother!!!!!!
I am expecting a call.
*(She slams down the phone, stumbles over to bed, and falls on it
and is very still. She weakly lifts her head and croaks.)*
See how she is?
Now do you see what I have to live with?
(She sits up.)
Fine, Fine.
Because when I'm eighteen, I'm out of here.
I'm just going to get a job and buy my own house.
And if I have enough money left over I'm getting my
nose done.
This is a mistake.
(She gets up to display her nose.)
See if they could just lift it. Just a little *(she does)*.
And then I'm having my boobs reduced, because these are
frightening.
This is from vacuuming.

(She goes over to mirror and complains.)
And I am so fat.
Look at this. *(She shows the fat on her legs.)*
Look at this. *(She turns and shakes the fat on her tush.)*
But I figured out this really great way to lose weight.

I can eat whatever I want and then I just throw up after-
wards.
It's so easy. I just go up to my bathroom and run the water, no one can even hear me.
I've already lost six pounds and I'm going to lose twenty-
five more and then I'm going to be so skinny.
Then I will have a boyfriend, because I just want a
boyfriend.
I wish Stevie was my boyfriend.

We had the best time last night.
(She sits on edge of chair.)
See, we were all hanging out and Stevie comes over to me
and he goes,
"So, Sandra, do your parents have any pills?"
I said, "Sure."

So I took him up to my mother's bathroom and we took
her lithium.
So we're in my parents' bedroom and he pushes me down
on their bed *(falls onto bed)*.
And he goes, "So, Sandra, you ever give a blow job?"
"Sure, hundreds of them."
Not that I had given hundreds of them, but whenever my
girlfriends come over for slumber parties we practice do-
ing them.
You know, like on hair brushes . . .
Not the bristly side . . .

But I just didn't feel like it, so I said,
"Well, Stevie, I'd love to, but I'm on a diet."
And he acted like I hurt his feelings, and he was going to
leave.
But he turned off the lights and he comes over and he
gets on top of me and he starts undressing me.

family secrets

I said, "Stevie, just a minute, just a minute."
And he goes, "Just relax . . . just relax."
It was hard, because his breath smelled like Southern
Comfort and egg roll.

But I didn't want to say anything because I didn't want to
hurt his feelings again.
And he starts undoing my pants.
I wanted to get a rubber out of my father's drawer, but I
figured, just this once.

So we were doing it, and it kinda hurt, but I didn't
want to say anything because I didn't want to hurt his
feelings again.

And it was only for a minute.

And he rolled off and he said, "Wow, Sandra, you're the
best."
I don't even know what I did.

(Phone rings and lights come back up. Sandra leaps off bed.)
I'll get it . . . Mom, I'll get it.

Okay.
(She practices saying hello.)
Hello . . . hello. . . . hello.
(She picks up receiver.)
Helloo.

Heidi? . . .
Heidi . . . I'm expecting a call.
You saw him. Where?
With Stacey?
So, why are you telling me.
Oh, you think I care?
Why would I care? So.

You did? You got tickets for the Amputators?
I can't. I'm grounded.
Okay, okay . . . I'll meet you at the Log in a half hour.
(She hangs up and plots.)

Mom *(gentle voice.)*
Mom?
Can I go out with Heidi for a little while?
Please, mom . . . *Pleeeeezzz?*
Mom . . . come on.
I know, but I'll try and be nice.
I hate you.

(She is propelled across the room and she is pissed. She remembers something behind the bed and goes to it. She pulls out an aluminum fire escape ladder. It is all tangled. She does her best to untangle it, loudly.)

Nothing. Nothing!

(She goes over to the mirror and examines her looks. She picks her face. She exaggerates her fat face and recedes from the mirror.)

What's wrong with me?

(She goes to bed and curls into fetal position. She pulls out from under the bed a bounty of junk food and eats it passionately. She hears the mother call. She quickly replaces the food.)

What? *What?*
Okay. *Okay!!!!!*
(She gets up and steadies herself and begins her exit.)

I have to go down and unload the dishwasher and dry the dishes.

family secrets

I started working when I was fifteen. I worked for my uncle Paul. He had created his own business in the midseventies by writing a newsletter that predicted the success and infiltration of cable TV. The business started in his house on Sally Lane. He would write the newsletter, then the whole family, his two daughters, my aunt Florrie, my mother and brother and I would stuff his media insights into envelopes, moisten them with a sponge, seal them, and send them on their futuristic way. Soon the envelopes took over the house and he moved to an office building in Rockville Center. I went too. I got out of school at three and I took the bus there. I was useful in the office because I could type. I learned to type in high school at the suggestion of my father. "If you can type, you'll always have something to fall back on."

I loved working at the office because I loved office products: new pads of paper, boxes of pens, cases of Correctotype, colorful paper slips. I loved business machines, the amazing and multipurpose Xerox machine, the scriptotype, which printed all the addresses on the envelopes, the mean and vicious folding machine (if you were not careful, it would chew up not only the newsletter but your fingers as well). I thought I had found my destiny. I would be a secretary. Well, I'd really be a poet, but to support myself, I would helm an office.

I had a nice paycheck and I put some away. At the same time, my uncle, who was also a predicter of stock futures, invested money for me. By the end of high school I had saved close to five hundred dollars, but my uncle had grown his stake for me to four thousand dollars. This would be my college money. At least the first year's tuition.

I would leave for college in California on August 19, 1978. I was one of the few kids leaving the SUNY system to go elsewhere. I was afraid. I didn't know anybody in San Diego—that was part of the reason I was going there. But I had a detour first.

In April of '78 my mother decided, with the assurances of Dr. Goldman, that she had rebalanced her chemicals so she could get off lithium, a lifelong dream for her. But her abrupt withdrawal from the medication that had kept her neurons in check for six years and had become a crucial part of her maintenance was dangerous. She devotedly went to Goldman for adjustments, but she didn't see the train coming from the other direction that was about to slam into her. It was my grandmother.

The relationship between my mother and my father's mother was a tenuous one. Because my mother had lost her own mother so early in life, Rose became a surrogate. Not an ideal surrogate, but she loved my mother in her own destructive way. Now, with my upcoming departure to college, my parents' decision that they too would be moving to California within the next fiscal year, and her other son Gary's recent departure to Maryland, my grandmother resorted to desperate tactics. She tried to kill herself.

She swallowed a bottle of aspirin, slit both wrists, and stuck her head in the oven. She didn't die. Was this a cry for help? The ambulance took her to Montifiore Hospital in the Bronx. My father spoke to her on the phone at the hospital after they revived her. He asked her what had happened.

She said, "I tried to kill myself."

He said, "Ma, you live on the thirty-third floor, why didn't you just jump out the window?"

She said, "It's too cold."

My mother found her new calling; she would be my grandmother's salvation. When my mother shifts realities she is convinced she is the Virgin Mary. She believes that her power and her connection with God give her special saving superpowers. It would be that driving energy, her withdrawal from lithium, and the obsession with being a savior that would put her back in the hospital.

One spring morning I was getting ready for school. It was my last semester of high school. She was in the backyard, doing some sort of a grotesque ballet dance all around the patio. She invited me to come out and see what God had created. It looked like a bunch of sod and bad landscaping to me. I declined. She was gone. I made myself a ham sandwich, threw in some Wise potato chips and a Coke, and got on the bus to school. When I got home the house was spooky quiet. Happy was mopey. I called my aunt.

"I'm sorry," she said, "they had to take your mommy to the hospital." I hung up the phone and collapsed on the linoleum. I was so angry and scared and hurt. I wasn't four, but I sure felt like it. This time I could fight back. I could scream and curse and take a lot of sedatives. My mother would call from the hospital and ask me if I believed in God. I said, "No." She would call me a whore and hang up on me. We skipped Passover that year. None of us believed in God anymore.

Fortunately, this visit to the hospital lasted only four weeks. They got her back on the lithium and she fell back to earth. She crashed. When she's high, it's like being on a bullet train. It takes a tremendous toll on her nervous system. She came home wiped out. I was glad to see her, but I wouldn't trust her ever again. My grandmother came out of the hospital too. I would never trust her either.

What kind of goddamn role models were they? A lunatic and a suicidal manipulator. Who would teach me to sew, to garden, to sing, to cook, to create a home, to care for my body, for my soul? I ached for the feminine to rise from me with some sense of herself intact. I searched for the phoenix.

I left for college on a Wednesday. My family drove me to the airport. I was scared, but I knew somehow that if I stayed in New York I would go crazy or die, probably both. When we said goodbye at the walkway to the plane, I held my mother's hand until the last second even as I walked away. I cried walking down the windy corridor. I wasn't sad, I was free. This airplane was my magic carpet. I had no ties, no image, no past.

sherry glaser

I picked San Diego, not because it was a banner school prized for journalism, my intended major, but because when I visited the campus while investigating all the California state schools, all the students were lounging about on the lawn and it was 75 degrees in December. I wasn't going to college, I was going to year-round summer camp.

My cousin Jack picked me up at the airport. I stayed at his house in L.A. for a week before being relocated to my permanent address. I would be staying at Zapotec Hall on campus. It was an all-girls dorm. I was bummed that I couldn't get into the co-ed dorm. I thought girls were boring.

I walked into room 205 on a Monday morning. My roommate had already moved in and she had taken the left side of the room. I plunked my stuff on the bed and scrutinized her bulletin board. It was covered with pictures. There was one common person in all the pictures. It must be her. Shit, she was a blonde—a skinny, gorgeous, probably native California blonde. I was depressed.

Diana walked in while I was hanging my good old reliable lion and tiger posters up on the wall. She was blond all right, but she had gained weight and looked healthy (well, not too healthy—we both could drink and smoke with alarming regularity, but we were young and resilient) and strong and friendly. She wasn't at all my stereotype of a California chick and I didn't mug her as she expected a native New Yorker would on the first day. We became best friends. We were both late our first day of school because of the rigorous party schedules set up by the fraternities in their frenzy to capture the minds and livers of all incoming freshmen. Diana would rush a sorority, but that wasn't my style. I was still a New Yorker and I never really felt comfortable in a group of cute and severely skinny giggling sisters.

I loved college. I felt so free, so autonomous. I went to class with bare feet and bellbottoms. I was the hippie I had always wanted to be. I dated my first black man. He was a prince from

Senegal. He was the first black man I had ever spoken to. I called my parents in a rage over this. "Why is it that I'm eighteen years old and I'm just interacting with black people for the first time? I find that very disturbing." They had no answer, but I could hear the fear seeping through the long distance lines. I didn't spend a lot of time on my scholarly education. I was bent on learning about life.

I met Billy in a creative writing class. The first day the professor instructed us to go over to someone in the class and introduce ourselves. I went over to Billy.

He was beautiful. He was part Blackfoot Indian, about six feet two, huge smile, daring blue eyes, smooth olive skin. We slept together pretty soon after we met and began our dramatically creative, but ultimately destructive relationship.

The following semester Billy became jazz critic for the *Daily Aztec,* the university's daily newspaper. He recommended me for the job of theater critic. We had a great social life, paid for by the paper, but we were critics. Our job was to be critical and it couldn't help rubbing off on everything.

He was taking a class in comparative literature, called "Drama in 3D." The first hour of the class they would read literature and . . . discuss it. The second hour, they did improvisation. I had seen a show in San Francisco during one excruciating vacation with my parents. I was amazed that the performers could take a suggestion from the audience and immediately incorporate it into a scene. I thought it was magic.

One night Billy came over to my dorm room after class and told me he had to do a Remprov, a rehearsed improvisation. Would I help him? I was skeptical but somewhat interested and always tried very hard to please my man. He wanted to do it to a Frank Zappa song titled, "Titties and Beer." He would act out the song and I would assist him.

He wanted me to wear a T-shirt with a picture of naked breasts printed on it. He wanted me braless. I'd come in on my cue and "shake my breasts up and down" and say, "I got me three beers and a fistful of downs and I'm gonna get ripped, so fuck you clowns." I looked at him in astonishment. He wanted me to burst into a room full of strangers and a professor at the university and throw my 38 D mammaries around and shout obscenities. He said it was art. I said No. I was furious that he would ask me to do such a thing—on Yom Kippur yet. He was persistent and offered me all kinds of sexual favors, so I agreed, but I wouldn't wear that stupid T-shirt. It would be a T-shirt of my own choice.

I was nervous. I waited in the hall outside the classroom. I wore a plain red T-shirt. Occasionally a group would come out in the hall and rehearse their scenes one last time. I watched them. They looked at me curiously. I obviously wasn't in the class, why was I standing in the hall? Then it was my turn and they understood very well. The students sat there with their mouths agape. The song was over. I think people were applauding, but I bolted from the room and ran back to my dorm. Billy called me later.

"Where did you go? You were great! Jerry wanted to meet you."

"I hate you," I said. "Jerry, who's Jerry?"

"The professor."

I met Jerry soon after. He was very tall, about six feet three, thin, bald, with a very prominent nose and thick, dark-rimmed glasses. He looked like a cross between Groucho Marx and a huge duck. I found him very attractive. It was his energy and this wonderful gift he gave us in the classroom. And his voice. It was like a honeyed viola. He was thrilled by my performance. I thought he was talking about my tits and maybe he was one of those professors who liked sweet young students to snack on. I was wrong. He was a devoted father to three beautiful kids and a wonderful husband too. He wanted me to take his class the

family secrets

next semester. I did. It was as if somebody finally turned on the light in my dark. I liked the first half of the class all right, reading Shakespeare and Molière, but it was in the second hour that my soul danced. Finally, after nineteen years of misery and worry, self-hatred, and depression, I got to play.

I could be anybody: a journalist; a murderer, a spy, a Tupperware™ saleslady; anywhere: a plane, an elevator, Democratic National Headquarters. Accents came: English, Spanish, Russian, Japanese, French. I was a child, a teenager, an old woman, a man, a French prostitute, in nothing but a teddy, teaching the class how to eat a strawberry. I was fearless. Jerry would choose me for his partner just to work with me. Every scene was real to me. Every word I meant. When class was over, I couldn't leave. I couldn't wait for the next Wednesday.

I took "Drama in 4D," but there was no 5D. Billy had become the editor of the arts section of the paper. He'd climb up on a chair and recite my latest grammatical faux pas and humiliate me in front of the entire newsroom. He also told me, one night in a parking lot after a lovely walk through the science building, that I had no business being a poet. That hurt. I'd been writing poetry my whole life. It was something I just did, like breathing. I broke up with him on the spot. I dropped out of school, I got a job at Western Union and I went underground. I found all the improvisation workshops I could. At the Marquis Public Theater I met Whoopi Goldberg. We did lunchtime theater for the office crowds. I spent most of my time in Pacific Beach in Jaquie Lowell's class. That's where I met Monica.

Classes were held at the Oakwood condo in Pacific Beach. I was nineteen when I walked in there. I was nervous, but like a junkie I had to get a fix. Jaquie had seen me at the Marquis, and she was happy to have me. She would become the greatest voice of encouragement to me.

Monica was new to the class. We made eye contact at the beginning of the class, but it went no further. Jaquie must have sensed something, because she put us together in our very first scene. It was emo spot. That is a game where you get suggestions of occupations, locations, and emotions. Once the scene is established by the players, sideline coaches freeze the scene and call out new emotions to move the story. We were given only a location, a supermarket. The first thing that happened was our carts crashed into each other. That was an omen.

There was a sultry chemistry between us. Playing with Monica was the most natural thing I'd ever done.

I was living in a garden cottage on Villa Terrace in North Park. I headed the telegram delivery department at Western Union, supervising men who had been delivery boys for close to fifty years. They remembered the day when telegrams had been delivered by horseback. At night I would go out with Michael or Rick or Steve—didn't matter who, it was all about sex then. It was 1980 and sex wasn't a loaded gun. I was looking for love with my eyes shut tight.

Then I got a letter. It was on this wild stationery. It had four sets of voluptuous crimson lips at the top of the page all poised in different stages of a kiss. It said something about the weather and how nice it was to know me. It was from Monica. I thought it was sweet.

In college I took a course called "Sexism in the Social Sciences." I needed an elective and it was in the women's studies courses, so I took it. No political agenda, just convenience. That's where I met a student named Mary. She had long blond hair, cute, but definitely white bread, tall. She wore overalls a lot. She came up to me after class one night.

"Do you mind if I ask you a question?"

"No," I said.

"Are you a homosexual?"

"No," I said, stunned. "Why?"

"Because, you look like one."

family secrets

"Well, I'm not," I said, vehemently defending my sexuality. "Are you?"

"Yes, I am," she said, "and I was wondering if you'd like to go for a soda."

"No, I don't think so, but thanks." I scurried away like a cockroach when the lights are suddenly turned on. I raced back to the dorm and looked in the mirror for a long time.

It was hard to convince Mary that I wasn't a lesbian. She was sure I had some latent tendencies and she would do her best to motivate them. She literally chased me around desks to get me to kiss her. She said, "Once you kiss a woman, you'll never go back." She begged me, hounded me, and finally one night, just to get her off my back, I kissed her. It was the softest kiss I'd ever had. Her lips were like satin rose petals. But I wasn't in love with Mary and finally she got the message. I put that kiss in my pocket and put it through the wash a few times. I hadn't forgotten about it, but it faded, like my Levi's.

I really thought nothing of Monica's letter. When I saw her in class on Tuesday I told her I liked the stationery and it was funny that she should write to me when she'd be seeing me the next night. She just smiled. I thought she was beautiful. Soft brown hair, a sharp beaked nose, a little crowding of her teeth turned the front two out a bit. Searching and soulful green eyes. Lips that hung like an orchard from her face and a body of subtle but meaningful curves. She asked me to go out to dinner.

Monica picked me up in her VW bus. We went to a place in Pacific Beach for dinner and she told me about her twin, Jane, and her older sister, Sheryl, and her brothers and her mother and father. I loved listening to her. She made me laugh, she made me tingle. After dinner we went and parked and looked out over Mission Bay, which was really her front yard. She asked me if I'd ever kissed a woman. I told her about Mary. She told me she'd been writing about me in her journal and read me a passage. It

sherry glaser ▨

was entirely erotic. She asked me if she could kiss me. I said yes.
Wild horses collided with my pelvis. The kiss lasted about, oh,
half an hour. She asked me if I wanted to come in and spend the
night. I said I couldn't, I had my period. She laughed. She said
she didn't mind, but I couldn't handle so much intensity and intimacy while on my moon. I wanted to wait. She drove me home
and kissed me again. I galloped down the path to my house.

The first couple of times I had sex with Monica, I cried. The
tenderness was exquisitely painful. It was so slow, so deliberate,
so unplanned. Sex with men always had that ultimate obvious
goal; with Monica it was boundless. Breasts everywhere, something I had longed for since I was a baby. I got to suckle, and
suckle I did. Mama.

I had this amazing sense of emancipation. I didn't need men
anymore. I felt more confident, I felt beautiful, funny, strong. I
was in love with a woman and I needed to share my newfound
joy with my family.

My folks had moved to California in 1979, but some event
brought all of the family back to New York. I thought I would
take this opportunity to tell them about Monica. We were in a
midtown apartment. I told my mother first.

"Mom, I'm in love."

She said, "That's wonderful."

I said, "It's a woman."

"Oh," she said, "well, whatever makes you happy." She gave
me a hug and I went to talk to my father. We stood on the apartment terrace together. He told me he loved me. That would be
the last time I would hear that for quite some time.

"Dad, I'm in love."

"Oh . . . " He didn't seem too excited. He remembered when
I'd been "in love" before.

I was nineteen years old. I was working in the circulation department of the San Diego *Union Tribune*. I wanted to be up-

stairs writing features and columns, but you gotta start somewhere. So I was one of "Dixie's girls." Dixie was the grand lady of the phone room. She taught us proper newspaper phone call etiquette and thought herself a snappy dresser and a fashion adviser for her girls. I hated the job.

"Yes, Ma'am. Didn't get your paper today. I'm sorry ma'am. We'll credit your account and bring you the late edition on us. We're sorry for the inconvenience ma'am."

"Yes, sir, your paper was soaked in the rain. I'm sorry, sir. We'll credit your account and bring you another paper. Yes, sir. Sorry, sir."

I spent most of the day apologizing to people, and on Sunday mornings I had to start apologizing to people at five o'clock. I was not happy. It was also at this time that I was feeling restless with society and the arrogance of the time clock. I hated the bureaucracy, the traffic, the noise, the garbage. I wanted to leave society and live off the land. I decided to change my life drastically. I wanted to move out from the house I had rented with some of my college roomies. The place was nothing more than a constant excuse to have a party, and Billy was back hanging around and criticizing me. I went looking for an apartment.

I found myself on Louisiana Street. I prowled the sunny apartment complexes and saw a For Rent sign. I didn't see an apartment number for the landlord, but I did see a door open on the second floor. I climbed the stairs and knocked on the screen door. A stocky, dark, bearded man with sparkling blue eyes came to the door.

"Hello there." I told him I was looking for an apartment and I had seen his door open and did he know who the landlord was? Or which apartment was for rent? He said, "It's this one. Me and my boys are gettin' out of town. Would you like to come in and see it?" I walked into his world. It was pure male, and authentic Cherokee. He was part Cherokee and his wife had been a full blood. The walls were covered with snakeskins and

sherry glaser ⬛

arrows and pelts. He had antiques everywhere and amazing detailed carvings of wild animals on burls of redwood. He had made them himself. He told me he was sick of society and was going to claim some land that was his up in Oregon. He said he was looking for someone to go along and help with the kids and would I like to go?

I was stunned. I mean, I didn't know this man from a bullet hole in the wall. I would have to be crazy to accept such an invitation. It was then his kids came home from school. Two boys, two sweet wounded little birds, lithe and dark, with haunted big brown eyes. The pot was sweeter. Ray told me to think about the offer and if I declined to go on the trip he would tell the landlord to let me have the apartment. I left his Native American shrine and went back to my car. When I popped on the radio "Cherokee People" was playing. I sang along.

I called Ray the next day and told him I was interested in going, but I'd like to get to know him a little first. He was all for that. We became lovers pretty quickly. I wasn't in love with him, but he was pretty insistent and he had potent marijuana and whiskey. I was in love with the idea of him. He had eight brothers (I'd always loved the Seven Brides for Seven Brothers motif) and they were ragged and rugged just like their big brother. He was a Vietnam vet and I knew I could help him reconcile the pain of that. I loved his boys and I wanted to save them from a motherless fate. I was in love with the Indian connection. He was my ticket out of the city. I didn't realize how much the fare would cost.

I told my friends I was leaving town. Their jaws dropped. Who was this guy? Was I going to be safe? I trusted Ray and I would be with his kids. What could happen? I told my parents I was giving up the civilized world and they were very concerned. I told them that we would stop there on our way to Oregon and they could meet my new family.

I hadn't counted on Ray painting his truck and camper shell

✶ family secrets

in camouflage green. I might have had a moment of doubt then, but I ignored it. I packed a duffel bag and the four of us snuck up the coast, trying to blend in with the trees along the freeway. The truck, bought from an old buddy for a song and a joint, broke down at my parents' house. The engine needed to be re-built. It would take a few weeks. I was trapped in the downstairs apartment of my parents' house with this crazy soldier and his kids and my mother and father upstairs pacing the carpet to its backing.

I could sort of see the trouble. He was rude to my parents, burping and farting loudly in their presence. I was a vicious smoker and a rebellious drinker and he liked to paw at me. My father had been having problems with gophers eating up the roots of his ice plants, so Ray, trying to help, dynamited them with m-80s. I thought my father was going to hire a hit man just to liberate me.

Ray liked to have sex with the kids in the room. They weren't watching, they were sleeping, I hope, but they were always pres-ent. We only had one room, but I could never relax and enjoy the act. It was all for him. The car got fixed and it was time for us to go. My parents stood in the driveway with the saddest, most frightened look in their eyes, as if they were seeing me for the last time.

We traveled through the most beautiful land in the country, but I never really saw it. Ray would drink beer while he was driving and instead of stopping the car to take a piss, he would hold the empty can he had just drank out of and urinate in it, while he was driving. When we argued he called me names, ugly names no one had ever called me. I was a big girl, so I called him names back. But he called the children names. Disgusting names, harmful names—dummy and stupid and dickhead. Every word was a dagger to their soft underbellies and they would crawl into my lap and lay their heads on my constantly comfort-ing breasts. I would protect them and tell them how smart and

sherry glaser

strong and funny and bright they were. I would contradict every message their father sent them, and then I would start on him.

I knew I had to unlock his pain about Vietnam to get through the abuse and find his gentle nature. I knew it was in there. We were sitting under the stars in Twin Peaks, California, when I finally asked him about the war. He told me that story just wasn't going to be told. I pleaded with him, but it was buried deep in his crippled heart.

We did have some fun. We went fishing and camped out a couple of times, but mostly we slept at rest stops along Highway 5, because he was in a hurry to claim his land. When we got to Oregon, this huge parcel of land he dreamed of was nothing but a little house on a residential street near the Puget Sound. It was terribly disappointing, especially because there was someone actually living there who didn't seem to know about his claim and had no intention of going anywhere. Ray was depressed and I was really ready to end this relationship. The verbal abuse was building. I wrestled nightly with the demons of abandoning these boys. They were calling me Mom.

We were at a rest stop in Oregon when Ray proposed marriage. Well, he didn't exactly propose. He said. "Well, we'll go back to San Diego, I'll get a job, and we'll get married and . . . "

I said, "But I don't want to marry you." Filthy accusations flew at me like rocks. What was I doing all this time with him? Just using him, like his ex-wife? I knew he had his gun under the pillow; he slept with it there. My life was in danger. The kids were witnessing this whole thing. I was humiliated and terrified. I crawled into the camper bed and tried to gather my thoughts and my strength. Ray came after me and held me down with one arm across my throat and with his fist cocked over my face. I fainted. Somehow the night passed. When I woke up, I crawled silently out of the truck. There were people all around. I went begging for help.

"Please help me. I'm with this crazy guy and I'm afraid he's

family secrets

gonna kill me." The people actually turned their backs on me. I went to another car, again I was ignored or told, "I'm sorry, I really don't want to get involved."

Ray woke up and he came after me and dragged me back to the car, twisting my arm, with me still begging the strangers. He threw me in the front and attacked me with violent language. He threw the kids in next to me. They held my hand. They were trying to take care of me now. We drove down the road. I was hoping someone might have gotten our license plate and called the cops and they would catch up to us soon, but no. Ray finally spoke after about half a dozen cigarettes. "Damn it, Sherry, don't you know how much I love you?"

I almost burst out laughing, but he probably would have killed me instantly. I said, "Yes, yes I do and I'm sorry. I will marry you. I don't know why I said no. I guess I was just scared." He took my hand and told me how happy he was.

We went back down the coast and I treated him like a fiancé. I was demure and sweet and surrendered to him at his demand. We even stopped at my parents' house. I told him I didn't want to tell them we were getting married just yet. Luckily, we were only there for one night. I said nothing to them. I thought I might endanger them and I didn't want any interference with my plan. We got back to San Diego and he dropped me at my old house. I said I wanted to hang out with some friends for the night and I would come over tomorrow. I disappeared for three months. I told no one where I was except my parents. He called them and insisted they tell him where I was; they politely refused and hung up. He couldn't find me and I was finally safe.

I never got to say goodbye to the kids. I never got to explain that they were not the reason for my departure. I had let them call me Mommy. I had tucked them in with sweet promises of the future and filled their dreams with the possibilities of a gentle world and then I ran away and left them to interpret for themselves my abandonment or worse the angry rationalizations of their father. I still feel the sting in my heart, but I had to go. Promises are a dangerous drug.

While I experienced the firsthand threats of my journey with Ray, my parents had weathered it along with me in their imaginations. It's easier to be going through the trauma than to be the one who loves the one going through it.

My father braced himself for my announcement.

"Yeah, I'm really excited. I never felt this way before. I know I've had relationships, but this one is really special. I want you to meet her."

I know it wasn't the most delicate way to put it. But what would be? My father winced. Maybe there was an instant when he considered tossing himself or me over the balcony. He told me he didn't think that was normal and he had a big problem with it. I was hurt by his response, but I had my love to keep me protected now and I got on a plane as soon as I could to get back to her.

In spite of my father's reaction, I kept barreling along. Even if he didn't want to confront my lifestyle, I would give him no choice. I would bring Monica up to the house to spend the weekend. My father would then witness how beautiful and charming she was and see for himself why I had truly fallen in love with this person. I didn't really ask my father. My mother said it was okay. I got permission by proxy.

Monica loved the idea of meeting my parents. She always enjoyed a good drama. We drove up the 101 in my little Datsun. At one point Monica was driving and we were singing and I had my bare foot out the window. Somehow we caught up with a bee and I got a seventy-mile-per-hour bee sting on my big toe. When we arrived, I limped into the house. My mother gave Monica a big hug. My father waved.

Norm was a good host. He was polite and sociable. I assumed that he had made peace with it, because he was really nice to Monica. My mother would occasionally alert me to the panic

family secrets

and anguish beneath his calm exterior. He never showed me a glimpse of it.

I imagine his imagination just went wild and he couldn't allow such fantasy to intrude on his very traditional, clean-as-a-whistle all present and accounted for inventory. I'm sure it didn't help that she and I were sleeping in the same bed and actually engaging in uncensored ecstasy. I had, however, unconsciously, thrown down the gauntlet.

My father didn't stop talking to me. He had a difficult time talking to me. He didn't want to hear about Monica. He'd change the subject every time. He'd much rather hear that I needed money for the rent than anything about my girlfriend. He didn't want to hear my name in the same sentence with Monica's. I didn't care or at least I acted that way, but the subtle and constant vibration of my father resonated in my nervous system. I pretended I was oblivious to him and I was too voracious for her physically and playfully to care about anyone else.

Our friends knew we were together, but we never officially announced it. The boys that had been flirting with either of us now took to trying to get us to include them in our favorite pastime. We weren't interested. Because it wasn't just us. It was a gallery of characters that came along with us. We were country western cowgirls, we were Irish Jews, we were Barbra Streisand and Barbara Walters. She was a rock star; I was a groupie. I was a hitchhiker; she was a lonely divorcee. I was her father; she was my mother. She was a Steve; I was Angela. We were biker chicks. We were friends. We were lovers.

I was still at Western Union. I would write Monica erotic telegrams and have my guys deliver them to her at the Italian restaurant where she worked in Old Town. I would have dinner there and she would practically give me my dinner for free as well as some very provocative suggestions for what exactly was on the dessert menu that evening.

The lease was up on my house and I had to move. I had no

idea where I was going to go. I really didn't have much money and I had become accustomed to living alone in an artistic, sexually private environment. I ran into a friend, at Dance Jam, a free-form dance experience on Friday nights in downtown San Diego, and I told her of my dilemma. She told me Whoopi was moving out of the canyon. I had been to Whoopi's place once, for a party after one of her performances. It was a cozy cabin on the edge of a quiet canyon in Golden Hill. I coveted that place. I called Whoopi and inquired about assuming the lease. She said I could have it, but if she ended up returning to San Diego, she wanted it. She never came back.

About that time, I got really tired of doing the club work. Don, who was in charge of the workshop and subsequent performances, was into very traditional casting. He was sure that the men were funnier than the women and so the guys had much more stage time. And the men we were playing with had a habit of casting us as wives, secretaries, ditzy bimbos. Not that those are entirely oppressive roles for women, but there are others, and we would have appreciated some variety and a choice in the matter.

The improvisation hovered at an extremely basic level. "Can we have a suggestion of a profession?" "Prostitute. Gynecologist!" So weary from all stereotypical and superficial comedy, I was determined to plunge into my real characters and those around me to present comedy with meaning and humor and even wander off into the forbidden land of pathos.

Nobody's sure who really started it. Monica and I were performing at the International Blend in North Park, and a hilarious performer named Maureen Gaffney would drop in now and then to play. Mo is of Irish descent and has the quickest, most consistent comedy presence I've seen. Robyn Samuels moved down from San Francisco around that time. She was tall and dark-haired, very witty, and could compose a coherent funny song on the spot.

The Hot Flashes were born in 1980. We were four very strong, unique-looking, funny, talented women doing original comedy, improvisation, and music. Kathy Najimy was coordinating performances at the B Street Cafe in North Park. It was a small women's cafe. She asked Mo if she knew two or three other women who might want to work out some comedy at the cafe. Mo asked us. Robyn came up with the name. We worked up two skits and an opening song, and a closing song and the rest was improvisation. We would play one weekend at the cafe, and if it went well, they'd book us again.

At the time my neighbor in the front house had a job driving a limousine. I asked him if he would drive us to our opening night performance. It was only ten blocks away, but he generously agreed. The limo was white and bigger than the cafe, and we felt glorious arriving there, with a long and luscious line of women waiting outside the cafe to see four women doing comedy.

It was packed. They literally sat at our feet. People were watching through the window. We made them laugh, we made them cry.

We thought of ourselves as feminist, but there was something universal in our work. Everyone loved us. I think it's because we started with a feeling circle.

A feeling circle is just what it sounds like. We all sit in a circle and one at a time we talk about how we feel. No one is allowed to say "fine." You must reach into your guts and find the emotion that is running through you and discover its origins. If you are in touch with how you really feel, you will create from a clear, intelligent, and aligned place. No emotion is taboo; the only requirement is that you are honest. I think we were. Up until then I dared not wander into such remote and unfamiliar territory. Identifying emotions when you've buried, disguised, and pretty much ignored them your whole life is like going back to kindergarten.

Once I got the hang of identifying and articulating my emotions, it was as if someone had flung open the curtain, pulled up the shade, and opened the window on a Technicolor world. I could see and breathe, and there was a chance I just might fly out that window. Feelings, for me, are the connection and cure for everything in my life.

We usually worked at my house in the canyon, draped liked Rubenses across my living room: Mo smoking Benson & Hedges out the window; Robyn and Monica dipping restaurant size tortilla chips in scalding Mexican salsa; me, eating chips too and occasionally sticking my head out the window for a drag on Mo's cigarette.

There was fertile ground for us. No one that we knew of was exploring the world of female humor, the office scenes, sister scenes, women's health, and other issues that affected our lives. One of the first and most successful scenes we did was the office party, where I played Gloria, a closeted lesbian. It was Gloria's thirtieth birthday and the gals threw her a party. During the course of the party the women swig champagne, open suggestive gifts, and try to fix Gloria up with every eligible man they know, until finally, from the combination of alcohol and giddiness, Gloria blurts out that she is in fact a lesbian. There is a moment of stunned silence, followed by the women expressing their fears and curiosity. The scene ends with the line "Gloria . . . I have a niece."

It was purely liberating to announce on stage that I was a lesbian, and of course the women's community responded in kind. Rarely had that word been used on the stage with such tenderness and acceptance.

It was during this time my private dichotomy became more severely pronounced. On the outside I was strident, confident. I

family secrets

took the stage by storm. But internally I was terrified, never sure that I had any talent at all. I was secretly competitive with my sisters on stage and dangerously self-abusive should I miss my mark or a brilliant improvisational punchline. I continued to do drugs, drink, and stick my fingers down my throat.

We played a scene called "Slumber Party." We were all teenagers, and the highlight of the evening comes when we all shared a deep, dark secret and finally sang "Somewhere" from *West Side Story.* We also sang songs that Robyn wrote. The Hot Flashes' theme song was "Come Out of the Closet":

> Come out of the closet,
> Burst through with a shout,
> With a little fresh air and a heck if I care
> We'll feel better inside out.
>
> Come out of the mad closet, the bad closet the
> orgasm I never had closet,
> the strong closet, the wrong closet, the
> I'd like to sing a song closet,
> the lazy closet, the crazy closet,
> the I don't smell like a daisy closet . . .
>
> . . . or "Bring Out the Womanside":
> Bring out the womanside, honor the womanside
> We all have a womanside
> Women and men
> Bring out the womanside, honor the womanside
> someday the world will be balanced again.

One afternoon during rehearsal, after the feeling circle and yet another jumbo bag of tortilla chips and salsa, Robyn, the quasi director of the group (mostly because she had her BFA in theater and was the oldest), suggested we do a scene about our issues with our fathers. I didn't have any issues with my father. Sure, everybody else did, but my father loved me.

About two weeks later, still without a "father sketch," we were performing at The Wing. We were doing "Office Party." All of a sudden I felt an excruciating pain in my lower back on the right side. I stayed with the scene and barely finished the show without collapsing (the only way I wouldn't finish a show is if I were unconscious or we were threatened with nuclear bombardment). When it was over I folded on the cafe floor and my friends drove me to the hospital.

After a thoroughly humiliating and agonizing pelvic exam by Dr. Total Stranger, I was diagnosed with a kidney infection and given enough medication to kill that infection along with any other infection within a fifty-mile radius. The next day, even with the medication, I was still in pain. I waved to my neighbor Mia as I hobbled down the cement walkway between our very intimate bungalows. She poked her furry head out the window.

"How are you?" News traveled instantly in Golden Hill.

"I'm in pain," I said. "It's a kidney infection."

"You should go see Bunny."

"Who's Bunny?"

"She's my therapist."

"Why would I go see a therapist if I have a kidney infection? Is she going to psychoanalyze my urine?"

"Just go."

So I did.

Bunny lived in the southernmost city in the continental United States—San Ysidro. It took thirty-five to forty minutes to drive there. Down through National City and Chula Vista on the way to the Mexican border. Her house was on the beach, an old gray saltbox, worn by wind and sea weather.

Her door was always unlocked when you got there. The light

family secrets

coming through the huge picture window in her living room revived one instantly. There were bunnies everywhere. Stuffed ones, cartoon ones, porcelain, magnets, posters.

I was pretty nervous when I got there. I said, "Hello," as I let myself in. A soft voice came sailing down the stairs. "I'll be down in a minute. Make yourself comfortable." I watched the ocean crash in and creep out until Bunny came down.

She was glorious. Everything about her was light. She had white hair, luminous skin, blue eyes rimmed by black-mascaraed lashes. Her flowering, generous body was clothed in a comfortable white cotton warmup suit. She looked cozy and ever so inviting. After she said goodbye to her previous client (who looked dazed but peaceful), Bunny motioned me upstairs.

More bunnies lined the narrow staircase wall and there were lots of photographs of all sorts of people. At the top of the stairs was her healing chamber. There was a combination of floor pillows and wicker furniture and, yes, more bunnies, and an altar with a statue of a beautiful deity and incense and another picture window that framed the Pacific Ocean and the ever-changing spring sky.

I sat across from her in a wicker chair. She looked at me and I forced a smile. I told her about my kidneys and, with the most benevolent smile I had ever seen, she told me kidneys hold our anger. And if I didn't deal with my anger, I'd probably lose a kidney.

"Anger?" I asked. "Anger at who?"

"Well," she answered, very gently but assuredly, "it's probably about your family. Your mother, your father, so on. Are you ready to deal with that?" I started to cry. It came like a river.

After a couple of sessions with Bunny, I was more curious about the issues I had with my father. I went to the Hot Flashes and said I was ready to explore my relationship with Norm. I first became my father through a dramatic exercise during which we literally (in our imaginations at least) got into our fathers' skins.

sherry glaser   ⚡

We made ourselves comfortable on the floor. We closed our eyes and imagined seeing the person we wanted to become. It had to be in a neutral place, like the park or a beach.

Robyn said, "Ask him if you may borrow his body for a brief time."

I ask him. The response, though uneasy, is a positive one.

Robyn says, "Now have him turn around and literally unzip his body."

I guide him gently around and unzip him from his head down to his toes and I ask him if I can climb in. Again, he reluctantly agrees. I put my feet in his feet, my calves in his calves, knees in his knees, thighs in his thighs, my hips in his hips my groin in . . .

"Wait a minute, not my groin in his . . . hold on . . . " We all jump out of our fathers' bodies.

Robyn explains, "If we are going to be our fathers, we have got to at least try to accept, try to imagine ourselves with penises."

"It's not the *penises,*" Mo said. "It's *our fathers'* penises."

We giggled and moaned for a while and ate a bag of tortilla chips and yet another jar of salsa before we could begin the exercise again. Finally after much coaxing and a few cigarettes, we go on.

"Groin to groin. Belly to belly. Chest to chest, face, hair. Throat to throat, there's the Adam's apple. Chin, lips, teeth, tongue, eyes, head, ears, shoulders, arms, wrists, fingers, heartbeat. Open your eyes and don't say anything," were Robyn's next instructions. "Just walk around. Move like him, walk like him, sit like he sits. Look out his eyes. Let his voice come."

It does, it comes. His twitchy eye, the way he sucks his teeth, sound comes, and now Norm is in the room with Lou and Bob and Jake. We are not comfortable with each other. Bob wants a drink. Lou joins him. Jake and Norm would rather have cheesecake.

We moved around and started talking about our jobs and the stock market, but our female daughter selves were struggling

■ family secrets

with these mysterious creatures who had such a magnificent presence in our lives but hardly any tangible offerings. We emerged from them exhausted.

The next time I "became" my father we had decided to do a full-fledged scene about a family stuck in an elevator together. (In fact, it's said the sign of good characters is if they can create comedy stuck in an elevator.) I took the role of the father.

Much of the time when we did a scripted scene in Hot Flashes, it was based on the experience of my life. I don't know if it was because my life was so colorful, if I was just more forthcoming with the information, or because I simply wasn't afraid of what my family would think if they saw the piece.

We chose the underlying issue of the scene to be a confrontation between the daughter and the father about "tickling." This is something my father did to me when I was a child. Tickling wasn't violent abuse, but it was confusing, and I always ended up wetting myself and feeling humiliated.

Usually I would go to Carmel for a vacation when I was totally broke to ask the holy father for a substantial financial investment. During one of my many sojourns in Carmel, I stood in the kitchen talking to my father about the Israeli and Arab dilemma. I said that the Israelis were responsible for just as much violence in the struggle as the Arab nations. He responded that the Israelis only retaliated and were acting in defense against the usually hostile terrorist attacks of the bully nations. I was simply trying to point out that there were two parties participating in the war. But his arguments grew more logical and glutted with his "facts." I turned abruptly and threw my silverware into the sink with a magnificent crash. I turned back and said, "You always have to be right. No matter what anyone says, you're right." I stormed into the guest bedroom, where I was ensconced, and slammed the door. He knocked apprehensively.

I knew this wasn't about the Arab-Israeli conflict. It was about us. It was about me trying to open a door to discuss things that

I knew about, feelings that I had. So in my awkward manner I finally got to bring up my resentment over the physical invasion of the tickling. He had no idea I had any feelings about that. He apologized and said he had never wanted to hurt me and I believed him and forgave him.

It was a mild enough trespass, but it was one I was definitely angry about and I had discovered it with Bunny. So it was a useful issue to present in our scene work without entirely alienating someone from the family. Monica would portray me, and confront me as my father. Robyn's "Joel" was based on my brother, a student of Tai-chi, and Mo played her own hilarious version of a mother.

It was during rehearsal for the scene based on that conflict that I actually experienced my father for the first time. We were rehearsing. We were standing around Robyn's piano and the dialogue was very intense. My "daughter" had confronted me and the family was standing around very uncomfortably. Mother was offering Life Savers and my "brother" suggested we all take a deep breath. Dad said, "I don't want to breathe." That moment was a bolt of lightning. I tumbled into my father's consciousness, free-falling through his pain. At once I had a visceral experience of his confusion and struggle and his terror of confronting anything that even remotely suggested he had been wrong, or the possibility that in his actions or thoughts he had hurt someone. I was devastated. I stopped and I cried. I realized that for the past year, every time I walked through his front door, I had delivered so many challenges to his psyche that he nearly collapsed. This giant, this patriarch who had withstood crisis after crisis. The alcoholism of his father, the illness of my mother, was blindsided by his little girl, his *hija buena*.

This, of course, gave a wonderful depth of color to the character. I felt extraordinary power doing this scene. That is, until I had to go to Carmel to perform.

Ever since I got into improvisation my parents had been a

huge support. My mother believed in it emotionally and spiritually, but my father was the one who wrote the rent checks when my career didn't generate enough money to cover the bills. Whenever I requested funds, he'd give them to me, but there was an underlying power struggle neatly attached. As long as I was calling and needed his support, it was more difficult to confront the issues that came up for us. I sold myself, a little, for the privilege of living an artist's life. But now I was taking a private issue between us public and not only doing it by impersonating him, but doing it in his face and before everyone in his community.

Hot Flashes drove to Carmel in a huge rented van. We rolled into town and went directly to the radio station, WKZU. J. T. Mason was going to interview us and get the ball rolling for our gig at Monterey Peninsula College. We'd perform there, but we were all sleeping at my parents' house. As we got closer to the station in the quaint seaside village of Pacific Grove, I started feeling sick, grumpy, and nervous. The girls were teasing me about "Daddy" and how I might get into big trouble now. I was sweaty through the interview, especially when it came to questions of how my father might react. I had no spontaneity. Everyone was funnier than I was, and I was pissed.

By the time we arrived at my father's house, I was in a state of terror and fear and insecurity. I was afraid of him and of his reaction. He was acting happy to be host and the king of the harem, but I felt there was something going on, something he was keeping from me. So I let the demons in my head run.

There was a huge crowd at MPC. My father and mother were producing the show and my father had contacted everyone in the city personally and insisted they attend. My aunt and uncle, my grandmother, all my parents' friends, everyone who worked in my father's office. Everyone at the performance knew my father. This was his show.

I was scared. My improv was unreliable. I was supposed to end the musical comedy number with a spontaneous song and include the name of the musical supplied by the audience, but it completely left me.

The music that cued the elevator scene started and I took a long, deep breath. I entered the scene as my father, picking my chin and talking his talk. People guffawed. I was sweating profusely in my red garage attendant uniform. (We all had different colors. They were really depressing outfits, but we sort of matched and they were cheap.) I could feel myself psychically leaning on my sisters to complete the work and stay with his body and voice, his character. We held the scene and it really was brilliant. Because the scene was so personal, everyone could see that it mirrored their own lives, their own tragic comedy, their own family. My father didn't seem upset. In fact, he was on cloud nine because we had sold out all our shows and I could pay my rent.

At this point I was sure that Monica was my true love and we should spend the rest of our homoerotic lives together in bliss in my canyon retreat. I asked her to move in with me. There was a slight shift in her energy, almost unperceivable to the untrained neurotic eye. Her retreat began at that moment.

Monica seemed to be avoiding me, so I confronted her one evening after rehearsal. So I said to her, "What's going on? Are we going to live together?"

"No," she said. "I want to see other people too. I'm bisexual." She went out the next day and came home with a boyfriend. Not just some sweet guy from down the block—this guy was an officer in the U.S. Navy. He flew F-14s. This guy was as far away from lesbian land as humanly possible. What could I do? I decided that I was bisexual too.

I, did, however, find a sweet guy from down the block, a nice Jewish boy, a folksinger named Jeffrey. I wasn't in love with Jeffrey. He was in an improv group we played with now and then.

family secrets

He was meek and mild and I could pretty much control the relationship, but I wanted Monica. I had her, too. When she finished her evening with the well-starched lieutenant, she'd come to my bed. I waited for her. Some nights I threw Jeffrey out when she arrived. I was constantly dizzy; performing, teaching improv, having a relationship with a woman and a man and taking a lot of drugs on my days off. I did, somewhere along the way, develop feelings for Jeffrey, but it was mixed with ownership and some sort of personal dependency. At least I had *someone*. And Jeffrey wrote songs for me. Love ballads that he would sing in Balboa Park or at Drowsy Maggie's Cafe. I loved that. But my attraction to him was something I had to manufacture. When we made love, I'd close my eyes and think of Monica.

Monica got tired of military life and dismissed her enlisted man. I thought he might kill her in a passionate rage, but he decently and quietly surrendered. It had been a struggle for him being with her too; she was untamable. At the time it happened that the house next to mine became vacant and Monica moved in. She would be my neighbor. My head danced with Sapphic fantasy. Then, miraculously and coincidentally, she was attracted to Jeffrey. This posed an interesting situation, and in the flexible, experimental eighties, it opened up all sorts of possibilities. So we tried them all. I was opposed to such co-mingling, but Monica was persuasive and so was Jack Daniel's. We tried sharing each other, but somebody always felt left out. On the nights that she spent alone with Jeffrey I would be wracked with obsessive anguish, listening for their footsteps down the walk, or even on occasion following them.

I figured that she'd eventually grow tired of boy games, but what I didn't expect was that Monica and Jeffrey would fall in love and run off together. Well, they didn't exactly run off. I mean they lived next door. But I lost them both. I had to sit in my cottage and listen to the exotic mating song of both my lovers calling to each other. It seems they had sex all the time

sherry glaser ▣

and always next to an amplifier. I was in Pain, major pain with a capital P.

I didn't believe that Monica loved Jeffrey. I felt she just wanted ultimate control of my life. I confronted her about her behavior and her abandonment of me and told her that her true nature was to be with me, and that she truly was a lesbian. She slapped my face, hard. I was reeling not only from the blow but from the loss of all things soft and kind and playful and beautiful. I was a lone lesbian. I began to prowl.

I started seeing Sarah and Grace and Rita. I needed to fulfill someone's needs and fantasies. I could be everything Sarah, Grace or Rita wanted. Never mind what I wanted. I loved no one. They loved me and that fulfilled the requirement for a relationship. I became an expert in being the "one." In every interaction I looked for the same satisfaction that I had with Monica. It just didn't exist. How could it? How could I see it even if it did emerge from this emotional quicksand? We lived next door. I saw her every day. I worked with her. I smelled her rose-scented skin. I craved her lips, but they were Jeffrey's lips. He had now written more songs about her than about me.

Rita saw me in my perfection. She is the one who convinced me to teach improvisation workshops, which turned out to be a haven for my creativity and my desperately fragile ego. She was in love with me. I needed to be worshiped.

She was quite overweight, so she also gave me an opportunity to confront my terror of fat. I thought by embracing her I could exorcise my lipid demons. Then I had a brilliant idea. I suggested that Rita become director of the Hot Flashes. She had a great sense of theater and timing, she knew us all so well, and, most importantly, she would work for little, or on occasion, nothing. Sarah was our lighting technician, so when we went on tour I was surrounded by three women with whom I was presently, or had been, intimately involved. I still wanted Monica, and Sarah and Rita wanted me. When it was time to go to sleep, the tension hung around me like a supersaturated shroud. I had to make agonizing decisions of exactly where I would lay down my exhausted and confused sentiments. If Monica would permit it, I would go to her. Sarah was always open to me, but she was very young (well, she was almost sixteen) and my sisters looked heavily upon the fact that I was consorting with a minor. But Rita was the most demanding, and she expected that I would be with her.

She was forty-two, nearly my mother's age, and she liked to have her way. She reminded me of my grandmother. For some reason—maybe guilt, maybe an unrelenting addiction to drama—I brought her home to meet the family.

My parents were shocked by her visage. The whole situation was unbearable. I decided there, in Carmel, that I would tell Rita I wasn't in love with her and refuse to sleep with her. She was in no-man's-land. I had created a very painful farce. Right before we left Carmel, I sat myself down on my father's lap and asked him how he was feeling about all this. He said he was very uncomfortable. I asked him if he hated me and he said yes. In a way I felt satisfied; I'd finally gotten a visceral reaction from him at Rita's expense. She wouldn't talk to me for the whole five-hour drive down the coast. I dropped her off in LA to see her daughter, who was my age and who could possibly give her some insight into my loathsome behavior. Then I went to a Jack-in-the-Box, ate a lot and threw up at a gas station off Highway 5.

Rita, however, may have saved my life. She introduced me to the church of Inner Christ. It was a metaphysical church, which taught that Christ or the God being was actually inside of you. No priest, or rabbi, just your own connection to God. It was scientific too. There was a specific prayer, with certain steps by which you could attain the desires of your soul. It worked in order of this acronym: TRUCAFTR.

1. Title: Naming the thing you desired, clearly.
2. Recognition: Recognizing the higher being, the eternal love and light, the source.
3. Unification: Unifying with that source, God, power.
4. Claiming: Claiming your desires, wishes, prayer.
5. Accepting: Accepting that which you have asked for. It is already yours.
6. Forgiveness: Forgiving the people or things or circumstances that seemingly were in the way of your having your desire.
7. Thanks: Gratitude for the reception of the gift.
8. Release: Letting go of the prayer and knowing it is so. And so it is.

A lot of the work had to do with affirmations; statements that redefined your reality. Repeating these affirmations would supposedly make them come to pass. I had affirmations all over my dressing room mirror and I repeated them as often as I breathed. *I am a worthwhile person. I am loved. I have no need to impress anyone. I simply express life and love.* It worked. I wanted to heal, this time as a conscious participant. I wanted the answers that would explain my weaknesses and I wanted them fast. I wanted to take on my life and my power and become whoever I was meant to be and drop all this ridiculous addiction and abuse. I had to go to the source.

I called a summit meeting with my mother. I would tell her everything about me and I wanted to know everything about her. Everything.

I told her I wanted to meet in neutral territory. She was in Carmel, I was in San Diego. We chose the Hilton at the L. A. airport. We met around noon. There were double beds in the tastefully decorated faux Laura Ashley suite. We lay on separate beds and stared into the disturbing mirror. So much had passed between us with no analysis, let alone confrontation.

family secrets

I told her about my life. I revealed all my secrets. I told her about the drugs and the cutting school and my violent introduction to sex and the years of self-abuse of bulimia. She was amazed. She had no idea who I had been or who I was. I laid myself down in front of her completely exposed, and with each revelation my soul creaked open a little, letting in this light that finally shone on my real self. The freedom was thrilling and terrifying all at once. Then I asked questions.

"Mom, did you want me? Did you plan to have a baby? How did it feel to have a baby so soon? How was I as a baby? Did you have enough money? Did you worry? How was I treated? What were the rules, the restrictions?"

They had not planned me, she said. I was the result of a faulty diaphragm. She was twenty years old. She ate a lot of liverwurst and mustard and pickles. (Hence my primal cravings for salt.) She said she was drugged for the birth and didn't have her glasses on, but she was awake. She said she didn't know how to raise a baby, so she went by the book. Every woman's mentor, Dr. Spock. Although he had never birthed a baby, he was the expert.

The first and most important rule was breast-feeding only every four hours. Definitely not on demand. Even in the face of her weeping, wailing, hungry child, she would wait for the tick of the clock to give her permission to fulfill her instincts. Rule number two, the baby sleeps alone. Of course, I was in my own crib in my own room and it was routine (according to the doc) that if a child cried when put in that crib, in the dark room, let it cry until it fell asleep.

We ordered food in the middle of this avalanche. Nachos and potato skins. I ate the whole plate along with my pain. After dinner and a few more golden revelations of my childhood, we both fell asleep. I woke up about eleven-thirty, kissed my mother goodbye, and drove home. Halfway between San Diego and L.A. I pulled into a 76 Station and threw up, on purpose. By the time I got home to the canyon in San Diego, I was furious.

sherry glaser ▣

The anger toward my mother was infantile. My next session with Bunny, I remember the sounds of that baby issuing forth from my lungs. I screamed, and the words that accompanied these hollers were *Please, please, somebody hold me, somebody come, somebody listen. I'm hungry. I need somebody, please.* But nobody came.

This rage had no end. I couldn't forgive her. I had twenty-two years of resentment in a vault. I had a right to be angry. I had a responsibility to be angry. It was my job. That unexpressed anger had fueled my self-hatred, my bulimia, my drug addiction and craving for cigarettes and Jack Daniel's. The simple truth was, I wanted my mommy. Letting go of that pain immediately would have launched me into a wild, unknown identity. I had nothing to replace it with. I allowed myself baby steps. I had to start at the beginning and nurture and repair the damaged psyche. So I bought myself a bottle.

No one told me to buy one. I was in the neighborhood Safeway and I just happened to be in the baby section. My hand reached out and grabbed a plastic nurser; I think it had little duckies on it. I got a bottle of Welch's grape juice and walked home.

I filled the nurser, put on my big fuzzy slippers and padded around the house sucking on this deeply comforting, pacifying rubber titty. The sucking motion and the need to look up to the ceiling to get the most potential from the bottle propelled me into my child, and the safety of that motion began the reclaiming process of my soul.

Soon everyone wanted my bottle. I mean I sucked it a lot—whenever I felt the need or desire, or I was just thirsty. I began giving bottles as birthday and Hanukkah gifts.

I called my mother and told her I couldn't speak to her. She understood that I needed time to sort everything out. I got deeply into my work. I was teaching improvisation classes and I had everyone call forth their mothers, including the men in class. I wanted everyone in the same boat with me. I had them.

family secrets

Everyone who experienced the exercise came out with rage or disappointment or both. They also came away with a sense of compassion for dear old mom, and potential for a really good monologue. But the overwhelming common denominator was that no one there, or anyone I knew, for that matter, had had a happy childhood. No one's mother matched their ideal or the instant-pudding mothers that we were spoon-fed from the TV. We was robbed.

Few chose to confront their mothers on these issues. "Too scary," they'd say, or "She'd kill me," or "I wouldn't want to hurt her like that." Even though they had received the random emotional and physical blows of the mother, everyone would protect her to the grave. I wondered what there was to lose. The abandonment had already been perpetrated; she really wouldn't kill them or couldn't. But the fear of losing the mother is immobilizing, even though she is already gone.

I don't blame my mother for these mistakes. Her past is much more disturbing than mine. She unintentionally brought her pain and guilt and unconscious behavior right along with her. But to heal these ancient wounds and affect generations ahead and back and to go on to my higher purposes in life and not keep revolving around on the same karmic wheel, I needed to confront my mother and claim my life. Saying "You hurt me, you lied to me . . . You left me . . . I won't allow you to . . . Do you remember the time? . . . Why did you? . . . Why didn't you? . . . Don't ever . . ." makes room for "I need you. I've missed you . . . I've always wanted to tell you. I wish I could have . . . I love you." It is a primary sense of liberation to be able to talk to the mother, really talk. Still, in that confrontation, she may have chosen not to speak to me, yell at me, deny my reality—regardless, the words got spoken and were the liberation to my reality, and it was the truth and therein lay the healing.

It was in the weeks following the confrontation with my mother that I chose to reveal my bulimia.

I went to the Hot Flashes first. I said I wanted to do a scene about women and eating disorders. Robyn challenged me on that saying that it really wasn't such a big issue after all. That floored me. Every woman I knew had some complaint about her body or fear about gaining weight. The issue was, and still is, epidemic. I said, "It is to me—I have bulimia." It was near impossible to convince them that I had it. They had known me at least two years and I was so good at it there was no clue or trace. Monica even asked me to prove it. I wouldn't. I just needed to say it. In the confession the power of doing it was diluted. After eight years of purging and destroying my body, I was finished. I wanted to live. Robyn wrote a song called "Greed" about our obsession with food and how we look. In the vignettes of the song, Mo overate and felt fat and bloated; Monica was an exercise freak and every move she made was measured in calories. And me, well, I was sitting at my typewriter, frustrated with my work, so to comfort myself I ate and ate, and then I turned my back to the audience and went through the motions of vomiting. It was one of the most difficult things I've ever done on stage, but it may have saved my life and a lot of women would come up afterward and thank me for that particular moment in the show. I had my bottle with me at all times.

Bunny was critical to me in this phase. My sessions with her concentrated on the places in my body where I had stored the emotional pain connected with my mother. Her sensitivity allowed her to home in on these places (especially in my back, which symbolized support) and with gentle and focused hands she coaxed the pain from me. Soon I could speak to my mother and share little pieces of my life again. But I was no longer her little girl. I was still her daughter, as I would always be, but I was her equal and, at times, even her teacher.

Because of my courage in confronting my mother I gave her one of the most important gifts of her life: the courage to confront *her* father. Her mother had recently died in a mental hospital, where she had spent the last forty years of her life. She never got to say all the things she had saved up over her lifetime to tell her mother. But she'd be damned if she'd miss this opportunity with her father. The next time she went to Albuquerque, she sat down with her father at the table and served up the truth. He couldn't remember anything of her allegations, but it didn't matter. She spoke. She was no longer the silent little girl with no power. She was a powerful woman claiming her experience, however rotten and devastating it was. Her healing began.

The Hot Flashes were invited to perform at the Santa Barbara Women's Music and Comedy Festival. It would be the first year the producers were trying comedy and they had heard of us. We were psyched. A four-day weekend in the lush Santa Barbara mountains and thousands of women, only women. Because it was exclusive, we had the rare opportunity to walk around in the summer breeze in the buff. This kind of naked opportunity inspires two things: the first is a remarkable sense of freedom and a thorough sensation of safety, but on the other hand, we feel a rage that we are not free to naturally expose ourselves, as men do on a regular, weather-permitting basis, without becoming instant victim pudding.

Men were not allowed, they only came on the land to remove the trash, and when they did their job, a woman would ride along with them blowing a whistle that warned us to cover up if we felt intimidated at having men see us naked. Nobody seemed to care. We were safe, surrounded by two or three thousand other women; they could stare but they couldn't touch us or hurt us. We were free and a lot stronger than they were.

In the flood of femininity, I suppose Monica was inspired. She teased me and flirted with me and we made out under the shade of an oak tree. It was such a relief to taste her again, to feel her body. I wanted to sit right down and cry, but it wasn't safe.

We looked into each other's eyes for a while. I could see her pain and, being the superhero that I saw myself as, in that pristine snapshot, I felt sorry for her. I could see how lost she was and still I thought I just might be her way home. We didn't talk about the digression. I just hoped we would happen upon more intimate opportunities.

As performers we were given yellow armbands that allowed us backstage. It was a great privilege. We got to go to the performers' tent to meet the music legends Margie Adam, Barbara Higbie, Teresa Trull, and a new punk voice coming out of the closet, Melissa Etheridge. We met Danitra Vance, a hilarious comic who ended up on *Saturday Night Live* for a while (she died recently of breast cancer at a sorrowfully young age). We were among the elite and it was intoxicating. The regular festival attendees, or Festees as they were called had to do some sort of work shift as a testament to the cooperative spirit of the festival. (The following years I attended as a Festee and had the assignment of guarding the land, or security at the front gate. I loved that job. I was the protector of three thousand women. I took my job very seriously and it is a job I would be honored to do again and again. It's Amazon work.) We only had to perform. The rest of the time was for entertainment, workshops, swimming, and tchotchke shopping.

I felt so strong there. So absolutely comfortable. It seemed natural not to see men at all. There was so much regard for each other, so much creativity, so much storytelling, spontaneous drumming and dancing, and joy and breasts everywhere. Long ones; short, happy ones; single ones; pointy ones; bulbous, eggplant-shaped ones. Black ones, red, white, yellow. It was a Breastival.

I was writing in my journal one afternoon, "I remember Mary saying I look like a homosexual. Now I see what she means. I'm solid with uncompromising features. I don't hide myself in make-up or binding clothes. I'm straightforward, direct, I walk tall. I just may look like a lesbian. I feel like a lesbian . . . Oh my God, I am a lesbian." It had finally come to me, a revelation out of that porcelain blue sky. Clear and unclouded. I am a lesbian. I stood up and saw Sue, our wizard of the piano. She was a lesbian.

"Hey, Sue," I called.

"Yeah? Hi, Sherry."

"Sue . . . I'm a lesbian."

"Great," she said, "that's great." She waved and kept walking along. I told Robyn and Mo the next time I saw them. But there was Monica. We'd been through that before. We had a show that evening and I hadn't seen her for a while. She showed up close to show time. I told her I was a lesbian. She was distant from me the rest of the festival. She was angry.

"Why do you have to label yourself? What's the big deal?"

However, seeing this as a moment of epiphany, I went out to experiment with my new lesbian wings. I saw her at an improvisation workshop. Eve. She was wild, like a banshee. Wild, thick wheat-colored hair. Strong bronze body. Marbled jade eyes. Great dancer.

After the workshop I introduced myself and we walked for a while, till we found ourselves on the grassy knoll by the nightstage where Hot Flashes would be performing the next evening. It was a gabfest. We had everything in common. We agreed about nonmonogamy and the necessity of dance and the complete protein of the avocado. I told her what was happening with Monica, my frustration of being with her at this all-girl fest and having to respect her hands-off policy until or if she initiated physically. Eve was open and sympathetic. We talked for two hours and we tried to find each other all during the festival when either of us had a free minute.

Monica noticed a lag in my attention toward her and that I was actually smiling and feeling good. She inquired as to the source of my joy and I told her I had met a woman. All of a sudden she was much more available and much more affectionate. I was too young and too naive and still too addicted to her to see the manipulation. I would suck on any bone she threw. But now I had Eve at the back of my libido. She was a tenured lesbian. I could be the new kid on the block for a change.

On the last night of the festival there was a full moon. All of the women gathered in the mother of all circles. There wasn't enough room for the thousands, so we did circles within circles. And we danced and chanted and claimed our power and it was a mighty music rising to grandmother moon. It was so hard to leave the women's festival. The security and the celebration with so many women is the healthiest medicine I've ever known. Eve and I kissed goodbye, nothing passionate, but sweet and inviting. We left the land of labias and went back to civilian life. Leaving the driveway of the ranch, we saw our first man speeding by in a pickup. I couldn't help but feel my heart sink as it recognized the ever-present and occasionally violent battle of the sexes. It was a difficult adjustment, the reindoctrination to fear and persecution. It's boring and time-consuming always to be on guard.

Eve and I wrote to each other immediately. Then one night, about a week later, there was a knock at my door. It was her. She couldn't wait to see me. We were in bed pretty soon after that. Making love with her soothed me and woke me up to the breath I'd been holding since Monica. She stayed a couple of days. Long enough to get introduced to my life and the people in it. Then she had to go back to work. She was a house painter in Carmel. Our phone bills were astronomical. My poetry exploded with her. She was the door to nature for me.

She had a motorcycle. A Kawasaki 500. A big bike, but she could handle it, and I felt very sensual on the back of the bike, with my hands around her waist. We'd ride through the hills of Carmel and she took me higher, to the Sierras.

I'd never really been in the woods. I grew up in New York and spent a week or two each summer in Connecticut visiting friends, but it was a lake, not a mountain range. Eve took me to the wilderness. We piled up the "Black Cat" (as we called our sleek transport) with the tent and bedrolls and some food supplies. It was a long trip.

When you ride on a motorcycle, you are particularly sensitive to temperature changes, especially on the Northern California coast. In the morning when we left, we were all bundled up in extra leggings and sweaters and leather; a couple of hours later, when the sun came out, we were drenched in perspiration and had to dismount and undress; but when the fog set in an hour later, we were freezing again and had to stop and dress once more. Then it started to rain. I hated everyone in a car.

We arrived in Eve's playground. She had grown up camping in these hills, knew all the trails, and trusted her body in their embrace. I, however, was tentative with each step, afraid of every little noise and suspicious of little creatures just wanting to make my acquaintance. I was awestruck by the magnificence of the forest and the redwoods, the stars. I envied Eve's easy familiarity with nature and she was thoroughly entertained by my awkward introduction to the Great Mother Earth. She took me to a place she called the Throne. It is a huge boulder that roosts above miles of luscious canyon carpeted with groves of redwoods. It is a view of forever and there is a naturally carved seat in the boulder where one can sit and meditate on the sky and earth for hours.

Eve took me to a cave. I had this cartoon image of a cave, one that presents it as a large carved-out hunk of earth that you can just walk into, like in the Flintstones. No. This cave was a hole in the ground, a good-sized hole. A hole that a woman or a large beast could climb down into. I wasn't sure if it was such a good idea, but I wanted to be inside the earth pretty badly at this point, and since I had Pocahontas with me, I figured I could trust the divine.

She climbed in first with her flashlight blazing through the dark tunnel. I followed immediately after. The smell was musky, primal, animal. Suddenly, after a few steps down, there was a cavern. Our flashlights spied around. We were inside. I cried. I laid my body flat against the womb wall and rubbed my face in the dirt. I was home. The silence, the peace, the deep ache of all time was here. In her walls were crystals, jagged tools of witches and magicians to remind us of the natural command and magic of the earth. We harvested a few and thanked her for them. I want to be buried in a cave. I want to be wrapped in a light cotton veil and put in the earth tomb. I want someone to paint big red breasts on the ceiling of the cave and then I'll be fed through all eternity, back to the mother.

Hot Flashes was on an extended vacation and I took this opportunity to live with Eve in a tiny basement apartment at the bottom of a gorgeous Victorian house in Pacific Grove. The top was classic, with turrets and elegant bay windows; the bottom had shoebox-size windows, so it was primarily dim and mildewy and musty, but I had my love to keep me dry and warm. The place was decorated with sacred stones, feathers, blankets; it was as if we lived on a altar. We painted houses together in the day and danced at night.

Under the microscope of living together, what comes into focus rather quickly are the annoyances and discrepancies that distance disguises, especially if the distance has been 350 miles. Eve's sexuality turned out to be much different from mine. She was more into the spiritual union of sex, the higher bonding, like looking into each other's eyes and melting, than the carnal, nasty, face-in-your-crotch union I was craving. I could see a combination of those two energies being mighty satisfying and I was willing to tread in her waters, but she wouldn't jump into mine, as she once had. I felt frustrated most of the time waiting for her to feel the perfect inspiration that would turn her on. I felt insecure and unattractive in response to her quirky rhythms and she had total control of the sexual realm. Even kissing was analyzed, measured to determine whether it was a true union of the souls or me just wanting to mount and hump her. I couldn't handle the pressure. Our relationship became mostly platonic, but we had enough going on in that department for me to rationalize that we would eventually achieve that perfect union. I mean I loved her after all, but my self-image as a lover suffered a blow. It reflected like a thousand mirrors around me and made all my insecurities march right up to the surface. I held on tight, but I woke up every morning anticipating disaster.

The physical oppression was the polar opposite of the freedom I felt with Monica. When I closed my eyes at night, she was still there. I would fantasize about Monica and the possibilities of still getting back with her, especially sexually. No one had ever moved me like her and the fear that no one ever would again was unbearable. But at this very moment, unbeknownst to me, Monica was falling in love with the man who would become her husband, James.

My parents' twenty-fifth wedding anniversary was on February 14. They were married on Valentine's Day 1959 and their song is "My Funny Valentine." To celebrate their twenty-five years together, they decided to renew their vows and have a big party catered with deli delights, my father's favorites, pastrami, knishes, corned beef, potato salad, cole slaw, kugel, and three flavors of rugeleh. It would be casual (my parents dressed à la country and western) and it would be held in their backyard. I was determined to be at this event with Eve; she and I had been together for at least a year. My mother, as usual, was fine. My father threatened to cancel the event, but with my mother's convincing and my pleadings he agreed Eve and I could come as long as we didn't touch.

It was a glorious day in the Valley. Relatives from parts near and far, as far away as Florida, had come to pay homage to the grand couple. My father's brothers, my mother's brother and sister, second and third cousins. Everyone from my father's office was there too. Old friends and new friends of the family too. Lots of people had seen my various performances, so I had fans there too. The rabbi was a young guy from the temple. My father was president of the men's club; he was very popular at the synagogue.

There was champagne and the unveiling of a twenty-five-year-old bottle of scotch. Eve and I forgot my father's golden rule (or maybe we didn't take my father seriously). We didn't make out in the kitchen or fondle each other in the yard, but when the bandleader struck up "My Funny Valentine" and had the happy couple waltzing around on the dance floor and invited everyone else who was in love to join them, we did.

He saw us. Everyone saw us. If anyone there hadn't known I was a lesbian, they did then. I took my father's moment of glory and I made it scandalous. I made it mine. I was being selfish. I wanted my relationship to be acknowledged by him and the rest of the world. I didn't see what the big deal was. He was angry and terribly hurt, but he went on, ever the courteous host. I had plunged a thorn into his side and he would be damned if I or anyone else was going to pull it out. He didn't stop talking to me, but I could hear the injury in his voice. Unfortunately, my gay pride and my politics made my only response, "Get over it, Dad."

When I got back to San Diego, I met James. He was like Jeffrey in stature, but he was much cuter and he was a musician too. He was on the brink of moving in with Monica, though she had just barely gotten rid of Jeffrey. I thought it would never last and I would soon be victorious.

⊠ family secrets

I had changed. I was calmer, a bit more confident. I was inspired by the confrontation with my father, although it had been painful for both of us. It was real. I felt nastily grown-up.

And something else had awakened on my recent journey. Something inside me was now set in motion to become the wise woman, the creator, the changer. It was the awakening of the witch. It was an ancient wake-up call. My soul was stirring, the link to spirit through nature. I had never had an experience of God before, but in the woods I knew it thoroughly and it resonated with the pagan belief that God, or spirit, is the earth herself and her energy connects us all to the truth, to the power, to the healing.

The truth about witches has long been obscured by wild prejudice. In reality they were leaders in the community. They birthed babies and they knew the secrets of physical, emotional, and spiritual healing. They cast spells, but with the intention of protection or ridding oneself of fears or anger, perhaps characterized as demons. These incantations were in essence a dramatic kind of prayer. Witches also used their psychic strength to change difficult situations. In fact, the term wicca, which is the original term for witches, means "to bend or shape." Some say they also had the ability to change physical shape themselves, and that kind of ability is honored and respected in many other cultures.

The damaging clichés that portray witches making evil potions and casting demonic spells were bastardized from the original reality of women working with herbs and plants to make medicine from the mother earth to heal. In the late fifteenth century the Catholic church, fearing the power of these women, began replacing the common midwife and medicine woman with doctors, soon introducing the notorious *Malleus Maleficarum,* "the Hammer of the Witches," written by the Dominicans Kramer and Sprenger. It implicated the gentlewomen as sorcerers, demons, and devils and began the gendercide.

sherry glaser ▣

I had a bumper sticker on my little red Toyota "My other car is a broom." I was reclaiming my real herstory and the painful herstories that became of it. I read all I could. *The Spiral Dance, Witchcraft from A to Z.* I learned to cast a circle, make an altar, and how to celebrate the pagan holidays of Samhain and Beltaine and the equinoxes and solstices. I kept my eye out for a coven, but my schedule didn't permit. I saw *The Burning Times,* a wrenching documentary depicting the horrors of the witch-hunts. While the Jews had suffered the loss of six million over the course of ten years, the victims of the witch-hunts suffered unspeakable tortures and nine million murders over four hundred years of persecution. The victims were women and children and many warlocks as well. It is astonishing to me that the trauma of the Jew is sanctified and kept holy, while the extermination of these women is relegated to a silly mask on Halloween. I must remember them and keep them holy as well. I am sickened by the images of witches that we perpetuate, the ugly noses and warts and the idiotic notion that they tortured children.

During this time I was teaching an improvisation class in my cabin. Ten students and myself would gather in the early evening to engage in sophisticated play that unearthed the unconscious, freed the child, and woke up the memory, the spirit. The warmup that preceded class consisted of stretching and relaxing. At the end of the exercise everyone would rumble their voices at the bottom of their bellies and bring them up into a loud roar getting all the frustrations of the day out in a cataclysmic bellow.

Jan, my neighbor, came over one morning looking worried and upset. She said, "Sherry your neighbor's baby died last night." I was shocked. She said, "Yeah, it was a crib death and they think it had something to do with you. That you're doing some sort of witchcraft over here and you did black magic."

I had to laugh. "Are you serious?"

"Yes."

I was afraid there would be some retaliation, that they would come over with a lynch mob. But my neighbors were so afraid of my sorcery that they moved out. I didn't know what to do. I did cast a spell then, that their grief would be gone swiftly and a new child would come in joy and they would forgive me and the loss of their baby.

Near the end of my tenure with Hot Flashes, I had an epiphany. It wasn't the-virgin-Mary-at-the-bottom-of-my-coffee-cup kind of an epiphany. It came from a stranger source, a dentist's wife.

One of my students liked me a lot, in that special way, but I had finally quit the silly habit of obliging every Tom, Dick, and Mary who took a fancy to me. Her real relevance to me was her connection to the spirit world. She had witnessed a channeling. Channeling is the ability to leave one's own physical body, through the crown chakra, the spiritual exit door, and allowing other spirits to take your place temporarily. A woman named J. Z. Knight, the dentist's wife, had started channeling an entity who called himself Ramtha. My student invited me to a special showing of a videotape of the event.

A beautiful blond woman entered the room and everyone stood up and applauded. She climbed onto a flower-studded platform and was surrounded by close disciples. She spoke for a few minutes and explained how she was introduced to this spirit. She had been making a school project, a pyramid, with her children. It was a long, involved process and by the end of the evening, she was exhausted and giddy. She picked up the ancient Egyptian symbol, placed it on her head and began to dance around. Little had she known that dancing is a primordial beckoning of the gods, especially if one's head is buried inside the tomb of an Egyptian king. It was then that the room filled with light and she heard the voice. After the explanation she began her meditation and allowed the spirit to enter her.

Ramtha was a benevolent, smiling entity. He had a huge smile and a deep voice that sounded otherworldly. He spoke. "Good day in your time, brothers and sisters. I am pleased to be in your presence on this day in your time."

He proceeded to speak in beatific platitudes. I was mesmerized by the vision of him/her. He went into the audience and without prompting would choose one subject and, introducing himself to them, would take their hands in his and kiss the top of their hands and then the palms. The compassion was so blissful, so healing that it would reduce the receiver to tears. One believed he could feel his subject's pain and immediately disperse it with some perfect wisdom to lift them from the strife they were convinced would be their ruin. At the end of the session he looked into the camera with eyes dark like an Abyssinian and said:

"Who are you living for? Are you living for others, pleasing everyone save yourself? Are you happy? Are you claiming every moment as your own, for your better, for your own good? I leave you now, brothers and sisters, but I am always there for you. I love you all." He left the body, and J. Z. returned, dazed and quite tired.

The next day I quit Hot Flashes. We had a summer booked at the Old Town opera house, but I was miserable. All the material that I had been introducing to the group was judged by Robyn as immature, unclear, and unusable. She was threatened because I had crossed the boundary into her territory: I had written a song. She said she didn't understand what the song was about, even though it was titled, "Addiction."

> Addiction's what I use when I choose to self-abuse,
> From beneath I deny the need to scream, laugh or cry,
> Saying no! with the power of my will,
> It's not myself, it's just the pain I want to kill.

family secrets

We sat in my living room ready to start a feeling circle. I went first. "This is very difficult for me, but I have to say it. I quit." Monica screamed. Mo said, "Yes!" She also felt the limitations of our stifling routine. Robyn threw daggers with her eyes.

I said, "I just don't feel good here anymore. We're not creating new material and I'm unhappy. I think it's time for me to move on." We sat in silence. We had been together four years. It was like a marriage and I had just said "I want a divorce." Robyn tried to make me feel guilty about my choice and my confidence wilted a bit, but my resolve was strong. There was general relief at not having to rehearse that day, of not having to conjure any more scenes. Our futures were now all uncertain, when just the day before we were in a secure and guaranteed position (at least for the next few months). For me there was peace in the unknown. Monica and I had talked about working together outside of the Flashes, but I guess she didn't believe that I would actually pull the plug on our respirator, or maybe she wanted the choice of when that event would occur. However, we were soon up in her living room, with her beloved, James, rehearsing. We called ourselves the Egomaniacs.

Egomaniacs, the time has come,
for us all to realize that we are the one.
Throw away the paper, turn off the TV.
We are what's happening. We chose our own reality.

Or our finale:

Now I turned out fine.
So maybe the world is a child.
Now I turned out fine.
So maybe the world is an angry teen,
or a woman coming to power.
You know what I mean?

Now I turned out fine.
So maybe the world is a child.
Now I turned fine.
So maybe the world is a wise old crone.
Or a spirit knowing forever,
I am forever, I am forever and ever and ever.

I was on my merry way, performing with the Egomaniacs, getting gigs in San Diego and San Jose and San Francisco. I was hardly paying the bills and if I couldn't pay the bills, I had to call my father and ask for money "for the last time" again. Not once did he deny me. He complained about it, but he never said no. I wonder if it would have done his soul such good to say, "You know what, Sherry, I don't approve of your life and I feel at times that you are purposely trying to hurt me, and since I don't feel love or support from you, why should I show *you* any support?" But my father's loyalty is unsurpassable. He loved me and would never leave me no matter what.

Eve moved to San Diego to be with me. It wasn't the happiest of times. She did, however, insist we put new sky-blue carpeting in the cabin, which was quite rank after years of traffic and the aroma of my three cats. She painted our walls "angora." It looked great, but it couldn't camouflage our misery. She was a bear living in the zoo and I was her keeper. It didn't help that I was the center of attention and Eve occasionally disappeared among the crowd. I also had to contend with the constant scrutiny of my now probably getting married heterosexual partners, Monica and James. They disapproved of the relationship. They disapproved of all my relationships and had a way of pointing out their shortcomings and making my choices in lovers seem idiotic, childish, and a waste of time. And I still had a small but visible candle burning in my heart for Monica.

Next time I did a show in Carmel, I planned to break up with Eve. When I decide to confront someone and express myself,

family secrets

there is nothing that can stop me. So even though Eve's dog of twelve years had to be put down unexpectedly that day, I still broke up with her on the way home from the vet. I figured she might as well mourn the loss of the dog and me all at once. Monica and James were proud of me. This was all-important. It was as though I was under some sort of spell because I saw them as having the ultimate heterosexual relationship. Everything they did was poetic and perfect; every other day he would bring her gladiolas and play the piano like an angel and sing to her. I couldn't have her and I would never find a man that could rival James. What could I do?

I sort of merged with Monica and James at this point. In fact, when they exchanged weddings rings, they gave me one too. It wasn't gold, like theirs. It was the prototype. In my symbiotic stupor, I accepted it, thinking this might also give me access to the nuptial bed. They had their wedding in the Colorado Rockies. I was the maid of honor and I also dressed up as Grandma Rose, an old Jewish character that I had just created, and sang "Sunrise Sunset." I stole the wedding, but I couldn't get anywhere near the honeymoon. Drat. But I knew they'd be coming home soon because we had to go to work and I would always have access to Monica there, because our energy and talent for improvisation and comedy were never even approached by James.

In the Egomaniacs, Bev, the character of my mother, was born. Monica played Miriam Nichols and I played Bev. Since Monica had James and they were married in real life, she got to play marriage scenes with him. My lovers weren't in the show. So Bev's husband, Ollie, was always absent. I flew solo, hoping that one day Monica would see the light and run off with me. This fantasy was still breathing because Monica and James were having trouble in one very crucial department: sex.

We did a scene where Miriam and Dickie went to a marriage counselor because they were having trouble with their sex life. I was the counselor. I was French. My name was Giselle. I tried to give Dickie advice on how to treat Miriam, but by the end of the scene, I had Miriam in my arms and I was kissing her passionately, just to give him the idea. Right.

So Bev and Miriam and Dickie had a New Age barbecue. We served the audience tofu dogs and frosted rice cakes. We still had a great following from Hot Flashes, but it wasn't as strong. We veered off in a selfish direction concerning only ourselves and our predicaments. It was group therapy on stage with New Age mentality and ideas. "Egomaniacs" was the perfect name.

The first time my mother saw Bev was in Santa Barbara. My parents had decided to fly down and surprise me for my twenty-third birthday. I didn't know my mother was in the audience and I felt really awkward afterward, but she seemed pleased, even touched, that I was using her character.

What I did in the Egomaniacs merely skimmed the surface of my mother's character. It was a caricature; it was Bev lite. I treated her mental illness like a joke. Bev being medicated and her skewed perceptions of life were merely fodder for Miriam's pity and punchlines. By the time I got to *Family Secrets*, Bev was a powerhouse of comedy and pathos who commanded respect for her struggle and her determination to heal.

About this time I met Greg Howells. He was a friend of James's. Greg and his wife had come to see Hot Flashes. Greg said that I met him after a show one night at the Old Town Opera House. I gave him a brilliant smile and sailed off in the moonlight. I have no memory of it. When we met again, he was in the process of getting a divorce and would be moving into the small, dark, cavelike room underneath Monica and James's house directly across from my house, about four feet away. Before he could move in, Monica and James had to get my approval because we lived so intimately and it was not unusual for one to lounge around in the buff.

He showed up one beautiful San Diego afternoon. I was sitting half naked in my living room writing a short story about a woman who wakes up one morning and finds her house has collapsed all around her and she has fallen into a hole. James knocked at the door. "Sheryl." (It always made me feel like a little kid when he called me Sheryl.)

"Yes," I said. "Come in."

"Gregory," he said, "this is Sheryl and these are her breasts." Gregory was awkward and polite. He had calm blue eyes and he said, "How do you do?" to all of us.

I said, "We're fine, thanks."

After he had the tour of the canyon and had decided that with my permission he would take the hovel, I went upstairs for the final inspection.

He said, "I've seen your show [the Egomaniacs]. I think you're great. I have a joke for Bernard."

Bernard was a character I did in a piece called Telethon. Monica and I would get a suggestion from the audience of a silly or serious cause that needed some good fund-raising. We would then bring out a host of characters, who would make up songs and routines about the issue. Bernard was a retired orthodontist trying to make his way as a stand-up comedian. He told the worst jokes, but his delivery was hilarious. He kept a cigar in his mouth with the wrapper still on it because, "My mother never took off her shirt to breast-feed me."

I said, "Okay, what's the joke?"

Greg said, "What's a dentist's favorite song?"

"I don't know, what?"

"Fillings, nothing more than fillings."

I laughed, I laughed a lot. It was funny and dumb and simple and sweet. I said he could move in.

He was studying to be a lawyer, just like his dear old dad. I didn't see much of him and I was busy making myself crazy with different women. But underneath the drama of these relationships and the show biz hubbub, I was really lonely. At the time I was reading a book that Monica had given me about creatures who had a deep, abiding need for a mate and a longing for union. The creature would send out signals or songs calling for its mate until one day the destined soul mate would appear. I started doing the same thing. I would lie on my bed and call out,

> *"I'm here. I'm waiting for you. I'm ready for you. Please come for me.*
> *I'm here. . . . Are you out there? I know you're out there some-*
> *where . . .*
> *Hello? . . . Hello?"*

I was outside my house one afternoon, cursing and crying about my night-blooming jasmine. Some evil aphid was devouring it and extinguishing my seductive night perfume manufacturer. There was nothing I could do. I sat on the stoop and cried. Gregory came walking by, heavily burdened with jurisprudence and contract law. He stopped and gave me his condolences, but I think he was smiling at the same time. The next time we saw each other I was defrosting my freezer with a hammer. He found that quite amusing. We chatted briefly, but our lives were on parallel courses, with nothing in common.

One afternoon, he and I were standing in my doorway musing about the weather and such, when I decided to cook some couscous and curried vegetables. I said, "Hey, want some?" He came in and we had dinner on my couch. We talked and we talked and we talked. It was like talking to a girlfriend. I don't mean he was effeminate, although he had a strong feminine side; he was just easy to talk to. It turned out we both liked racquetball and made a date to play.

I played racquetball in college and fancied myself a pretty strong player. I had been with women for five years and had no trouble showing my strength to a man; I thought I could and would beat him. I didn't, but I sure gave him a helluva game.

When we got home, Monica was spying out the window, just keeping an eye on things. I couldn't figure out why she was so curious.

About a month later, Gregory was late for our racquetball appointment. I hate to be kept waiting. If you call, okay, but don't just keep me waiting. I was furious when he arrived.

"How dare you? Do you think I have nothing better to do than to sit around waiting for some stupid shit like you?"

"I'm sorry," he said. "How can I make it up to you?"

"You can take me out to dinner."

And we went off in my little red Toyota to play. We were in the middle of a very intense volley when I smacked myself in the mouth with the racquet. The pain was swift and stunning. I dropped my racquet and howled like a baby. He came over. "Are you okay? Sher? Where did you hurt yourself?" Again I noticed that goofy smirk, as if something about this was entertaining. I pointed to my right upper lip and he put his hand on my shoulder and ever so gently and tenderly kissed me there. It felt as if an angel had done it. And then, as in cartoons when Bugs or Elmer gets konked on the head and sees stars dancing around in his noggin . . . I saw hearts.

I hadn't realized what had been going on. In my narrow search for true love somewhere out there, I didn't notice who was standing right in front of me. He was kind, considerate, funny, easygoing. He was fun to play with. We could talk for hours. He was my friend.

I'd never been friends with a man or a boy. They were always mysterious frightening objects; either I was under their control or I had them completely powerless. This man was my equal. As the game went on, I was a bit distracted by the fact that suddenly I found him attractive. I didn't want to start acting silly, coquettish or different at all, but old habits sure die hard. I struggled through. When I got home that afternoon I didn't want to say goodbye. I had planned to go dancing and thought I'd casually ask him to come. He declined, saying he didn't like to dance.

You know how when you're considering someone as a mate, you have that secret checklist. Everything the potential applicant says and does is scrutinized and filed away. Before the mating process, you could care less; now the slightest error is grounds for dismissal. Well, I almost dismissed him right there. Dancing is my connection to freedom; without it I feel imprisoned. But I had danced alone before, in fact, I preferred dancing alone, so I could forgive him. We did plan for dinner though, the following night.

We were having a date. I hadn't been on a date with a man in years. I felt funny but excited, like a little kid. We both showed up clean and casual and on time. He said if I wouldn't mind, he'd like to take me to Torrey Pines before dinner. He golfed. I got over his not dancing, but a golfer? We were doomed.

Torrey Pines golf course is located in La Jolla. Its cliffs gaze out over the Pacific Ocean. It's lined with cypress and eucalyptus trees and of course the torrey pine, the only tree indigenous to Southern California. It's gorgeous. We arrived around sunset, so we could just walk on without paying. I felt really nervous, expecting the golf course authorities to apprehend us immediately, but he was so calm and sure that I went along, only looking over my shoulder occasionally. Greg said walking on the course would be like taking a walk in the country. He was wrong. It was much more beautiful and dramatic.

We went over to the putting green and he threw some balls down on the perfectly manicured turf. He sank them from two, three, four, and five feet. We stood on the green as the sun escaped into the ocean. He stood with his putter in his hand and watched in awe. "'Rage, rage against the dying of the light.'" Ah . . . he quotes poetry. I felt the warmth of the sun enter me as it sank.

family secrets

We went over to the first hole. He put the ball on the tee and sized up the distance of the course looking out toward the flag. He settled down on his feet, brought the club up over his head, paused at the top, and came down in perfect form, through the ball, which went sizzling through the air, with a trail of smoke behind it, like a rocket dropping its boosters. He followed through, holding at the top. I was transformed instantly into a heterosexual. I wanted to mount him right there on first tee, but I really don't know golf course etiquette and thought it might be inappropriate. It was getting dark, so we walked to the car.

We went to Sam's Deli and got hamburgers and French fries. It was there, over the Formica, that I told him, "I like you, Greg. I mean I really like you."

He said, "I like you too. I really do." We ate our burgers with big grins on our faces and in our pants. He paid for dinner and left a great tip. I admired that. Then he took me to the movies. He took me to see *Pee-wee's Big Adventure*. I really didn't want to see that movie, but then again, I didn't want to go golfing either. As we were walking into the theater he asked me if he could hold my hand during the movie. I thought I was going to cry. I said yes, and he took it right there. He held my hand all night. Our hands fit so well together. They're about the same size, good strength in each. Mine's a bit softer, but not much.

I thought the movie was silly. Greg loved it, and by the end of the film, I loved Gregory. We went home. We walked down our cement path to our doors. I invited him to spend the night. He said, "No. This is really special and I don't want to rush in. I'd like to wait." He kissed me on the cheek and said goodnight. I went into my house and felt deep ecstasy. It was as though hot fudge was running through my veins, sweet and thick and loaded with calories.

It took a few more dates until he would spend the night with me. The first time he slept with me he wore his pajamas. We didn't have sex. He just held me and kissed and cuddled me. The tenderness scared me. I couldn't really let it in. I couldn't let my heart invest in this moment, because if I did and it wasn't really genuine, then I would surely shatter and die. I didn't know how to behave. I worried that he wasn't sexually attracted to me, but Greg said he thought I had a great body and I was truly beautiful. Not pretty but deeply, hauntingly beautiful. He just wanted to be close and hold me and love me.

The first time we had sex was exquisite. I'd known him such a long time, it was a quiet intimacy that built to a carnivorous passion. After a luxurious long time, I had a rip-roaring orgasm. I wept. He quickly apologized for hurting me, holding me tightly. My tears turned to serious laughter. How could he think he's hurt me? He had no idea that that explosion detonated my secret heart, my sacred wild emotions, and I felt free and safe enough with him to completely express all the pain and joy I had been storing up in my sexuality for over ten years. He thought it was just that his penis was too big, but no—it was just perfect.

The next morning after some brief coziness and kissing, I started the inquisition. The first thing out of my mouth was "How do you feel?" He said he was "Fine." Wrong answer. I tried to explain to him that I was asking for the emotion behind the "fine" curtain. He was stumped. Was this a test? I wanted a descriptive analysis of his inner experience. Again he said he was "Fine." We had a fight. I saw a light go off in his eyes and I panicked, but I knew that it was good to find out early in the game if he would play by my rules too. If not, I could shut down early and suffer only mild depression and only fleeting fantasies of suicide.

He left without breakfast. I got busy being afraid and building up a lovely coat of armor. But when I saw him later the flimsy shield dissolved into a puddle and we were in each other's arms. I wanted him and he wanted me and we would learn to navigate

family secrets

the snarled and treacherous paths of our lives that made us afraid and prideful and kept us from the possibility of loving someone without destroying them. No one we'd ever known acted in that fashion and we had no teachers, only our hearts.

My parents were thrilled that I had fallen in love with someone who had a penis. To top it off, he was in law school. They had hit the jackpot. He wasn't Jewish, but that was all right.

Monica and James were behaving like the evil neighbors next door. They threw disapproving glances over the banister whenever they had the chance. They sat me down and said that Gregory was dangerous, that he had a drinking problem, he was a gambler, he was not to be trusted, and I really shouldn't be sleeping with him. For some reason I thought they knew what they were talking about and began doubting the reality of my relationship and how I felt about him, or at least how I saw him. Gregory didn't give a shit. All of my other lovers had stumbled under their scrutiny, but he just flipped them the bird.

I knew he wasn't perfect, but he was entertaining and real. Every night before we went to sleep he would tell me a story. The tales were all so rich with detail and enchantment and so soothing I would never make it to the end. One morning I woke up and while nestled in his musky armpit I told him, "You're not a lawyer, you're a writer."

I hadn't planned on getting pregnant.

Monica and James had. They had been trying for months. It was a sore spot between them and was slowly becoming an obsession for Monica. We actually did a fertility ritual at Monica's house, where four of her closest friends took fertilized chicken eggs and cracked them over her head while she lay in the bathtub. Nothing was working. I kind of envied the freedom they had to have sex whenever they wanted and not be bothered with birth control and also be inspired by the possibility they were making a baby.

Gregory and I weren't practicing safe sex though. It was still early enough in the eighties that we were ignorant of the fact that heterosexuals could transmit the AIDS virus. We were lucky that neither of us was infected, considering our multiple-partnered past. We were using the basal temperature method of birth control. I had to take my temperature every morning. When I was ovulating my temperature would rise just a bit. I would make a note of it on a temperature chart and we would abstain from sex during the rise in temperature. I was advised to keep the chart for a few months to watch the rhythm of my cycle and see the common time when ovulation would occur. I stayed with it religiously for months, and then I got sloppy. I had misplaced my chart, so I started a new one and the calculations went awry.

At this point Gregory and I were struggling with our relationship. We were completely different people. He liked to golf. I thrived on emotional drama. I wanted to know the subtle beating of his heart. And Monica's predictions of Greg's addictions to drugs, alcohol, gambling, were true. There was nothing that would destroy us right away but we were laying a grand foundation for failure. There were the usual male-female tugs of war. I wanted more time together, he wanted more freedom. I wanted him to do more around the house, he wanted me to stop nagging and trying to control him. I said I couldn't handle this anymore without going to see a therapist. We went to Bunny.

To start the session she asked each of us one very important, very simple question: "Do you want this relationship?" He answered, "Yes." I answered, "Yes." She advised us to take care of our own personal shit and commit to the relationship and enjoy it. We went home and had great sex for days. It was then we conceived our daughter.

My period was a week late. I was nauseated. I was nervous. It was March 30, a Monday night. I know that because it was the night of the Academy Awards. We drove to Planned Parenthood in Gregory's big white Ford. Greg stayed in the waiting room and I went in to give some urine. I didn't know what I wanted to hear. The technician came in, and said, "Well, I've got good news."

I was relieved. I wasn't pregnant. "You're gonna have a baby."

I almost fell off the chair.

"Oh," she said, "is that not good news?"

"Uh, yeah, that's a . . . I don't know."

"Oh," she said. "Well, think about your options and let us know." She left the room and left me with my embryo. I laid my hands on my belly and cried.

I came out to Gregory with an awkward smile. He knew. He took my hand and hugged me. He looked scared. We paid for the visit and got back into the car.

He asked, "So what are you going to do?"

"I'm going to have this baby."

"Well, maybe you should think about it."

"No," I said, "I want it." I had taken so many chances in the past and never gotten pregnant. It was meant to be. I felt it. I knew it. I'd have this baby with or without him.

Monica was mad. She was really mad. She thought I did it on purpose to spite her. She quit the Egomaniacs. I was glad. Greg had been encouraging me to do my own show, and here was my opportunity.

I immediately began taking great care of myself. I stopped smoking and started eating properly, no drugs, no alcohol, no nothing. I became a saint. One night over dinner at the City Deli, I told Greg that he really didn't have to stick around for this if it was too much for him. I had a wonderful family that would support me and I would be fine. He responded well to my open-door policy. He was appreciative and said that of course the decision to have the baby was ultimately mine. Now there was no pressure and so he could examine how he really felt about the baby and about me. He was working as a waiter part-time and still going to law school at night and I could see the

sherry glaser

newly created responsibility lit a big fire under his already short fuse.

A couple of days later he said, "Well, we should probably get married."

I laughed. I said, "*Probably?* Ha! If you want to marry me, get down on your knees and tell me all the reasons why you want to marry me, and then, *maybe,* if I like those reasons and I can think of some reasons to marry you, *then* we'll get married."

He thought I was being a silly woman. I thought he was being an asshole. He didn't exactly get down on his knees, but over tricolor pasta at Stephano's, he told me all the reasons he loved me and how much, and it really seeped into my heart like a great sonata. He asked me to marry him and I said yes.

I started writing my first solo show. I would do characters that I had created in my previous venues. Bev, my father, Grandmother Rose, Miguel, and a southern belle named Sherylyn. I started making lists of the details of their stories, the pertinent story line, the comedy and the drama I wanted to include.

My mother's list consisted of her obsession with being the perfect mother, her nervous breakdown, her relationship with her mother, her husband and her children. My father's list was meager, because I couldn't get any information out of him, so I chose to reveal the trials of my sexuality through him. Miguel would represent my spiritual quest, Sherylyn would detail her pregnancy, and Grandma would reflect on love.

My friend Cindy Beryhill was doing a gig at a coffee shop in downtown San Diego and asked if I wanted to share the bill. I had forty-five minutes to fill. There was about a crowd of thirty or forty people at the cafe. I had a couple of props, a pair of glasses, a newspaper, a scarf. I became one character after another just by turning my back to the crowd. It was difficult, because they were all around me. I also danced for them. For some reason I thought they would find that entertaining.

Monica sat at her table with a frozen look of semi-approval on her face, a weak smile mixed with a sneer of envy. I tried not to look at her. I finished the evening with the Grandmother. People in the audience loved the work. I felt encouraged and determined to do it again.

My first trimester of pregnancy was challenging. I had some morning sickness, but I used the natural remedies I found in a Wise Woman's herbal book. I would chew on ice cubes of red raspberry tea and eat lots of almonds. It helped immediately.

I spent a lot of time cozied in our cottage nestled away from the traffic off busy Fern Street. It was a glorious spot in the city. I walked out on my balcony to see huge eucalyptus trees and bamboo shoots and tried to communicate with the little one blossoming in my belly. Most of the trees were draped with morning glory and hemmed with nasturtium and anise. We had snakes and hawks and lots of cats running around.

Francesca and David lived in the first house off Fern Street. Francesca had given birth to a son in '82. That would not be unusual except for the fact that she had had her baby in her living room. And what made it even more memorable for me was that during the late stages of her labor she invited the Hot Flashes to come up and say hello and do a number to take her mind off the rigorous struggle of labor. We sang our little hearts out for her as she huffed and puffed. A few hours later, after a concert of primordial grunts and screams that whipped through the canyon, Evan was delivered. I was impressed that Francesca had the courage and self-confidence to have her baby at home, and filed it away under Important Things to Do.

After the confirmation of my conception I realized that for all my years of education and high consciousness, I had no idea what was happening in my body. I wanted an immediate education. I went right to Francesca and got the name of her physician, who would support such a bold act of autonomy.

Dr. Paul DuGre was Canadian. He was a short man, close to sixty, with a gray mop of unruly hair and sad brown eyes resting atop droopy bags. He was in tremendous physical shape. He swam two miles every morning in the chilly Pacific Ocean. He had a modest office in Washington Heights, in San Diego. He was associated with Mercy Hospital and worked with a stable of midwives. He gave me a thorough examination: pelvic exam, blood pressure, blood tests, urine, heart. The tests came back and all was well. He gave me a list of foods I should avoid (the usual greasy goodies and sugar dandies) and the foods I should eat more of—fruit and lots of greens. He calculated my baby was due to arrive December 6th, Gregory's birthday.

Dr. DuGre had delivered thousands of babies, mostly at home. He was convinced that most of the C-sections going on in this country, as high as 54 percent in some hospitals, were the result of hospital interference. Not only would he be my and the baby's physician, but he also taught a class for mothers (and their partners) to educate them on the physical and emotional process of becoming a parent.

Classes took place in Dr. DuGre's living room. It was always a joy just walking through the door and seeing all these fat-bellied mamas sitting on elegant and comfortable pillows. The house smelled of sage and sandalwood.

Our first class was pretty gentle. We learned about the journey of the egg to and through the fallopian tubes and the amazing sperm brigade that has to enter the hostile acid environment of the vagina, which kills most of them immediately. Only a few of the clever and strong make it further than that, and only one heroic ambassador of existence gets safe passage to life. We witnessed on film the splitting of the fertilized egg. We watched it divide and divide again until it became an embryo, looking like a baby reptile, and then its radical and miraculous transformation to the fetus.

family secrets

We discussed toughening up our nipples so we could tolerate breast-feeding; that would be our partner's job. If you didn't have a partner, you'd have to pinch the little rosebuds yourself to prepare them. We discussed proper exercises for strengthening the pelvis and stretching the uterus. The doctor told us how the perineum (the hole into the vaginal barrel) stretches naturally (another fun job for partners is helping the perineum stay flexible with olive oil massages.) There really is no need for episiotomies, a routine procedure at hospitals, along with shaving the expectant one.

Dr. DuGre started his antihospital propaganda early, with gruesome tales of hospital births gone amok. It was his way of committing us to this home process and making us feel that the only safe place to deliver a baby was at home. His tactics worked very well. He spoke of the invasion of the fetal monitor, which, connected to a wire, is inserted up into the vagina and up through the *os,* the opening to the uterus, and placed on the baby's scalp to measure its pulse and vital signs, and the powerful Pitocin that doctors would routinely inject to induce labor if a woman was slow to dilate or past her due date.

Pitocin eliminates the early stage of labor, when a woman learns to handle the intensity of the contractions as they increase in frequency and impact. With the introduction of Pitocin, she's hit by a Mack truck in the uterus and will surely demand an epidural immediately, lose sense of the contractions, stop cooperating with the contractions and using them to open the pelvis, then volunteer passionately for a C-section. There are plenty of natural herbal alternatives that can move the labor along, even start it mildly, holistically.

He went on to explain the hospital procedure for the newborn. "When babies are born, they come out with a protective coating called vernix. It keeps the skin protected in their new environment. It is excellent skin lotion and midwives and aware doctors advise mothers to rub the lotion on their own faces and hands to soften and protect their own skin. Hospitals routinely scrub this off, leaving the baby vulnerable to skin infections. The injection in the thigh is vitamin K, and the ointment in the eyes is silver nitrate to protect the child's eyes in case the mother has gonorrhea. It is administered as a precaution even if the mother hasn't got gonorrhea. It is unnecessary. It's an overwhelming and painful introduction to life. Babies are then swaddled and laid in a plastic bassinet, all alone. And if it's a boy, there's a routine circumcision. . . ." I swore I would not subject my precious newborn to such violations and a monologue was born.

I gave it to Sherylyn, a naive country girl, who was impregnated by her beau, Bubba. She talked of all I had learned on this prenatal journey, complete with pictures and statistics.

I couldn't get any attention from the major theaters. They all liked Hot Flashes and enjoyed the Egomaniacs, but taking a chance on a one-woman show was altogether different. I felt shunned and hurt; after all, Kathy and Mo had played the Old Globe. I rented a bookstore in North Park called the Present Time. It was really a gift shop, and the proprietor looked as if he was on highly illegal drugs, but he wanted to get a performance space set up. Based on my reviews and my confidence, he rented me the space at the back of the store for thirty bucks, a big investment for me at the time. I worked religiously on the monologues, while Greg labored away in contracts class. I had a beautiful arras, a dressing screen, that I would put in the corner of the "stage" and do my costume changes behind. I had a boom box for music segues whose buttons I would push myself. I created the flyers, and distributed them. The show was called *Coping*.

I had a decent following from all my stage experience and my classes, those that I took and those that I taught. The newspapers were also kind enough to give me some mention. The first night all fifty seats were sold.

I was nervous. I waited upstairs in the loft and watched people file in, friends and strangers. Dave announced this as my debut performance. The audience cheered, and I walked out as the Father into their lovin' arms.

I wore a pair of reading glasses and an Oxford button-down shirt. I held a newspaper and used it to emphasize my points. I picked my face and sucked my teeth just like my dad. The problem was, I had very little information to work with. My father had been very stubborn.

"Dad, how did you feel when I brought Monica home, or when I danced with Eve at your anniversary?" He said, he had a "problem with it." I said, "Having a problem is like having a box. What's in the box?" No answer. So in his monologue he talked about his crazy wife.

"She loves to send flowers. Not just flowers. Balloons, and stuffed animals, and chocolate, and dancing gorillas. You know what my florist bill was last month? Two thousand dollars. She sent the florist flowers."

He talked about being happy.

"I lived in New York fifty years, no one ever asked me if I was happy. I moved to California, they ask me every day."

Next I became my mother, Bev. I wore a different pair of glasses and a scarf around my neck.

I was in the body of the woman I had come from. I could feel the tension around her cheeks, the quiver of her lips, the sound of her tongue coming away from the roof of her mouth. I felt her fleshy hips, her Buddha belly, the dry skin on her toes, the roots of her ever-changing colored hair, her inverted nipples. I could feel the remnants of Thorazine and Stelazine and shock treatments. I smelled of Arpège, though I never even came near a bottle of it.

I wanted to incorporate not only my mother's story of losing her mother but my own story of losing my mother. She had lost her mother when she was four. I lost her when I was four.

Then I did Sherylyn in pigtails and with a southern accent. I was four months pregnant. I came on stage with a pronounced belly and two books. I explained how Bubba and I got pregnant in the first place.

"We tried to use a diaphragm, but Bubba hated the taste of that stuff and one night while I was trying to put it in, it slipped out of my hands and went flying across the room and hit Bubba in the back. He put it on his head and started dancing the hora and singing in Jewish like that."

I showed pictures of the developing fetus.

"Even if you put a bonnet on that it's not gonna help."

Then I did Miguel wearing a bandanna around my head and a silver jacket that I had pirated from the Egomaniacs. Miguel, an enlightened Chicano, was based on my spiritual side. He came out with a can of lite beer in his hand and took a long pull.

"Here's to the light. It's great there's light in everything now. Beer, fruit cocktail. You know a miracle happened to me this morning. I woke up! Yeah! My eyes could see. My ears could hear. My lungs were pumping. I am alive! And you are too. And we should be grateful. Just think about how many people are dead. Not us. We are alive! And then you know what happened to me? I saw God . . . I looked in the mirror! All right!"

Then I did Princess. She was an early incarnation of Sandra, with loose hair and a big T-shirt.

"Do any of you have a job? Wow. Like, do you have to get up in the morning before ten o'clock? God, if I have to get up before ten I'm really cranky. I had this job being a waitress and it was really hard. I mean everyone is always telling you what to do and the customers always need something. Like, this one guy calls me over, frantically waving his arms, and so I come over and I say, 'What?' And he goes like, 'Can I have some water?' and it's sitting right over there, like about ten feet away. He can't even get up and get it for himself. People can be so lazy."

Then came Rose. I wore old-lady glasses and a button-down blouse.

They laughed, they cried, they stood up. Dave booked me for the next two weekends. I got a wonderful review in the *San Diego Union* and I sold out on the following weekends.

By the time I was five months pregnant I couldn't really perform anymore. The male characters started to look awkward with this protruding belly. I wanted to concentrate on me and my baby and my soon-to-be wedding. We had decided to get married before the baby came so we could have our honeymoon alone. August 22 would be the date.

The invitations were simple greeting cards with a charming illustration of children dressed up in wedding costumes and playing out the nuptials. The guest list was small, about fifty people. Monica and James were not on it. It was a painful decision for me to make, but an honest one. They had disapproved of our relationship from day one. The two of them were constantly criticizing him, and me for choosing him. How could I invite them knowing their scorn? And I still had too much competition going on with Monica to have the perfect relationship, and the perfect wedding, because hers and James's was so quintessentially storybook. I could never compete. They were very hurt, but even in our confrontations about my decision, not once did they withdraw their protests or ever acknowledge our joy and our desire to be married.

We wanted a simple wedding (besides the politics that complicate every wedding). It had to be inexpensive and what we couldn't pay for, I'd ask my folks to throw in. It wouldn't be much. The first thing I had to do was find the hall. I wanted something special. I remembered this quaint little cottage on the cove in La Jolla, perched on the cliffs of the Pacific Ocean. Greg and I took a ride to see what it was.

It turned out to be the La Jolla Bridge and Shuffleboard Club, where the elders of La Jolla would come and while away the hours shuffling little pucks across slick cement lime green courts. There was a lovely library/sitting room, with a piano and huge picture windows that looked out at the sky and sea. Adjacent to it was a spacious hall that had long tables and could easily serve as the reception area. It was small, but we were inviting only fifty people. I fell in love with it. I wanted it. Greg loved it too. I called the Chamber of Commerce and the rep told me I could rent the place on a Saturday night, but it would cost me. How much? I braced myself. "Fifty bucks," he said. I said I thought I could scrape it together.

My friend Judy the Beauty on Duty who owned and ran the Big Kitchen restaurant in Golden Hill would do the catering for about seven hundred dollars and I would bring my stereo. The whole wedding, including my dress (which I bought off the rack at Saks Fifth Avenue on sale, for one hundred bucks) would cost about a thousand dollars. That is, until my parents decided that they would fly in relatives the night before to stay at the Colonial Inn in La Jolla Shores, and they themselves would take a private plane down to San Diego. Then I think it came to ten or fifteen thousand dollars. My parents had offered to rent Greg's tux for the wedding too, but he declined, saying he would take care of himself.

We were getting ready in our glorious honeymoon suite at the Colonial. I didn't have any qualms about his seeing me in my gown before the wedding, so I showed myself off to him and felt like a blushing bride regardless of the fact that I was six months pregnant. I asked him to show me his groom attire. He disappeared into the bathroom and came out wearing a starched pair of blue jeans and a Brooks Brothers shirt. I laughed. He said, "What's so funny?"

I said, "I almost believe you would wear that."

He said, "I am."

I hit him. I said, "Forget it. If this wedding means so little to you that you would wear the clothes you golf in, I'm not going through with it."

He called his father, who was staying at an inn down the street. His brother would lend him a jacket and his father would provide a tie. He left to get dressed and I walked to the club with my family.

When next I saw him, he looked wonderful. He'd even shaved. The ceremony was pure and simple. My brother conducted the proceedings dressed in Japanese gi and called everyone to order with the ancient gong. Gregory and I stood before everyone and acted out our wedding ritual. First I told him all the reasons I loved him and why I wanted to marry him and then he told me. He then read a poem that he had composed for the occasion:

> I love you Sheryl, Sheryl dear.
> I love the fuzz upon your ear and when . . .
> I love your lips which like a rose
> soft and sweet and fragrant grows
> into a smile, which like the sun
> plays upon the world as one.

We exchanged rings. I had taken all the gold that I had in my jewelry box, necklaces and bracelets that I'd gotten for my sweet sixteen party, rings and earrings. I had them all melted down and there turned out to be just enough gold to make our wedding bands. The butterfly-shaped design was based on one of the Norse runes (an ancient system of divination—runes were symbols carved into stones used like tarot cards.) This particular rune symbolizes breakthrough, passage from darkness into light. It also resembles the sign for infinity, a sideways eight.

My father read a passage from the Bible he had gotten at his bar mitzvah, and George, Greg's father, made a toast to us. In the Jewish tradition, we had a glass wrapped in a cloth napkin, and in breaking with tradition, we both stomped on the glass. Everyone shouted, "Mazel tov." We danced to the music from my stereo, and ate and laughed. My uncle took pictures and we were happy. We went back to our suite and counted our gifts. We made about seven thousand dollars. I said, "We should get married more often." The next day we had the wedding breakfast and took off for our honeymoon, first in the angelic sleepy hills of Julian, California, and then in the satanic, erratic stimulation of Las Vegas. We had all that money, and we couldn't very well just put it in the bank.

I spent the remainder of the fall preparing for birth. I'd walk two or three miles every day, swim, dance, and go to a lot of movies. Greg took on more hours at the restaurant and began studying for his finals. Unfortunately for him, they were scheduled the same week the baby was due. In his uncompromising dedication to me and his newborn he would skip his exams and ultimately finish his ambiguous struggle to follow in his father's footsteps and walk his own uncharted path.

My parents had decided to come to San Diego for the birth of our baby. I was excited to have my mother coming to support me. My folks were staying at a bed and breakfast inn around the corner from our house. On my due date, December 6, I had a few Braxton Hicks contractions (preliminary contractions, little nudgings from the uterus, but nothing spectacular). Since it was Gregory's birthday we wanted to celebrate, but it was hard with the distraction of the possibility of labor literally kicking in. By seven o'clock that evening it was apparent there would be no baby, so we decided to go out to dinner and have a birthday party. I hadn't had alcohol or chocolate for eight and a half months. I was ready to explode, and I wanted some comfort. I had red wine with dinner and had a piece of the chocolate birthday cake. We said goodbye to my parents. My father had to leave in the morning to go back to work. I was sorry he would miss all the fun, but you can't hurry love. My mother would stay a couple of days and see if anything happened.

family secrets

We went home and got into bed. Greg massaged my perineum and we lay very close next to each other, our hands on my belly, feeling the marvelous undulations of this hesitant creature. We spoke to it. "Come on, baby, we're ready for you. Come on out. Mama wants to sleep on her stomach." We went to sleep.

I was awakened at three-fifteen by a very demanding cramp in my lower back. It lasted about fifteen seconds. Fifteen very *long* seconds. It was a contraction. I woke Greg up. He said, "Okay honey, I'm gonna time these," and went right back to sleep. I was annoyed, but I got up and got my pad and wrote down the time: 3:16. I went back to sleep too. Dr. DuGre had told us it was very important, if contractions wake you up in the middle of the night, that you should sleep between them, so you'll have enough stamina to go through the labor and delivery. I was awakened at three twenty-six. Ten minutes apart. I slept for ten minutes, but they were very intense contractions. I was getting scared, visions of giant heads and shoulders trying to rip through my perineum danced through my head. I woke Greg up again. He held me and helped me relax and breathe into the pain. Eight minutes apart, seven minutes, six. I called my parents at five-thirty and told them I was in labor and if Dad wanted to stay, there would probably be a baby that day.

At six-thirty the contractions were five minutes apart, and I called the doctor. He said it sounded like the real thing and he would send the midwife over. He said, "Meanwhile, do your exercises." I got up and hulaed and squatted. When the contractions came I would meditate quietly on my rocking chair and rock with the pain. It hurt, but it wasn't unmanageable.

Gerry, the midwife, arrived about nine-thirty and found me dilated three centimeters, a long way to go till the required ten. I ate organic strawberries, succulent treasures; they never tasted so sweet. Everything was magnified in my concentrated state. I drank red raspberry leaf tea, vital for relaxing the cervix. My

sherry glaser ▣

friend Carla arrived and my mother followed. My father waited next door at Monica's house. I thought this very kind of her, considering that once again she was excluded from another major event in my life. I had thought about having her at the birth, but the wounds still had not healed between us, and she still resented the fact that I was having this baby.

Kahari, aka Fern, is the messenger of birth. Her character is a combination of my New Age Goddess-worshipping self and the great mother that I am. It is her job to recreate the birth of our daughter in the most physically demanding twenty minutes I've ever done on stage.

> *Puts on a loose, Indian print dress, sits at dressing table and*
> *sings:*
> There is an old woman living inside, Watch her spin, see
> her fingers fly.
> She's the beginning, she is the end.
> Our grandmother, sister and friend.
> She is the weaver, we are the web.
> She is the needle and we are the thread.
> She is the weaver, we are the web.
> She is the needle and we are the thread.
> Everything she touches changes.
> She changes everything she touches.
> Everything she touches changes.
> She changes everything she touches.
> Changes, touches
> Changes, touches.
>
> *She lights the sage stick and smudges herself with smoke and*
> *rises from the vanity.*
> *Enters.*
> The moon is full tonight.
> You can feel it.

family secrets

(Turns in a circle and sends smoke in the four directions.)

My friend Molly is coming over to celebrate because we both get our periods on the moon.

(She puts out sage and places on end table.)

So we're gonna do a menstruation ritual.
See, we each have these hard-boiled eggs and we cradle our eggs,
and we thank them and we chant and we release them.
And then we eat the eggs.
And you know, since I've been doing this ritual, my PMS is gone.

And I don't know if it's the new respect I have for my body, or . . .
just the extra protein I'm getting from the egg.

I love getting my period.
Don't you?
I feel so connected to other women.
I think we should call it *fem*struation,
I'm *fem*struating.

Did you know that in the beginning people thought it was magic that a woman could bleed, and then heal, all by herself. They were the healers, they were the first doctors, and their medicines were herbs and roots, and flowers.
That was before the Bronze Age, when the female was worshiped as the Goddess, Quan Yin, Yemaya, Inana, Kali, SHE gave birth to all life.
It wasn't Adam's rib. It was Eve's vagina.
And when a girl first got her period the whole community would celebrate with elaborate feasts and ceremonies honoring her connection with the mother. But when I

sherry glaser ⚡

125

first got my period, my mother gave me a box of Junior Tampax and a jar of Vaseline and then I locked myself in the bathroom for an hour and a half *(puts leg up on chair and looks, as if trying to figure out where to put it)* until I figured it out.

(Takes leg down)

I hate Tampax and I hate those pads.
I just want to flow.
Miguel said he would build me a menstrual hut, so I can bleed in peace.
And of course I had my baby at home.

I wanted to feel my connection, my power!
I wanted to *be* the Great Mother!!
But it took me the longest time finding a doctor who would let me have my baby at home.
Let me!
I found one. Paul DuGre.
He told me that, "If you're prepared, having a baby at home is safer. Safer and healthier for you and the baby."

My first contraction came about three-fifteen in the morning.
Now, how would you describe one of those things?
You know what they're like?
Did you ever stub your toe on the metal part of your bed?
Well, imagine doing that . . . over and over and over and over . . .
for about twelve hours.
That is what a contraction feels like . . . and it woke me up.

(Goes over to the bed and lies down. Contraction hits and legs go up slightly in pain. Head rises too. She sits up.)

family secrets

Miguel? . . . *(hits him)* Miguel?

Wake up, I just had a contraction.

He said, "Okay, Kahari, you just relax and I'm gonna time these."

And he went right back to sleep.

I stayed up because it was important to me and I watched them go from ten minutes apart to nine minutes apart, to eight minutes, to seven minutes . . .

And finally, about six-thirty in the morning they were five minutes apart, so I called Dr. DuGre.

I said, "Well, I think I'm gonna have a baby."

He said, "Well you're probably right. I'll send the midwife over, but meanwhile, you do your exercises."

See, he taught us in his birth class that you can't just sit around and wait for your baby, you gotta help.

(She rises from the bed, pregnant.)

And the best exercise you can do to help the baby move along is the hula.

(She does the hula.)

See this opens up the pelvis, so the baby can just slide right out,

which is what I was praying for.

Then Geraldine arrived and she brought all her equipment, in case of emergency. She had one of those stethoscopes attached to a microphone, so when she found the heart tones, we could hear them.

(Mimes the stethoscope on her belly and listens.)

Swish swish, swish, swish swish.

What a sound.

Then she felt for the position of the baby, and the head was down.

She said, "Your baby is on the runway."

sherry glaser ▪

127

Then she did an internal to see how I was dilating.
She reached in and she felt my cervix was dilated three
centimeters.
That means that the opening to my womb is opened
about like this . . .
(She shows small opening with scrunched hand.)
But it's gotta open ten centimeters.

Then she said, "Kahari, you look so beautiful today and
this is your last day pregnant. You know, you should have
your picture taken?"

(Fern rises.)
I said, "Okay, I'll just run right over to Sears and have my
picture taken."
She said, "No. Just go out on the terrace."
So I went out on the terrace and Miguel ran to get the
camera. *(She poses.)*
But by the time he focused it, I'm having a contraction.
(She grimaces in pain.)
That's the picture he carries around in his wallet.

Geraldine heard this commotion, she comes running out
and she says, "Kahari, you're fighting the contractions. If
you want to have a baby, you gotta relax.
So when you feel the contraction coming, just take a deep
breath and say,
Oh well . . ."

That really helped, but I had to find the right position.
So I tried a couple. *(She bends over, clutching the chair.)*
Ohhh wellllll!
Not great. *(She stands up.)*
My favorite position was when Miguel was standing in
front of me and I could put my arms around his neck.
(She mimes it.)

family secrets

Ohhhh welllll!

When I was done I could see that he was sweating, and I thought, "You know, he's working as hard as I am but he's not feeling any of this pain, and the only way he would is if I got down and bit him on the testicles."

And I'm talking about every three minutes.

Then my best friend, Molly, arrived.

Molly and I had been through so much together, I wanted her to be the baby's fairy godmother.

Then my parents arrived and when my father walked in and saw me standing there naked, next to Molly, he walked out.

So, Molly and my mother held me up because Miguel was tired.

And they had me walk. *(She walks, holding on to their shoulders.)*

I walked about six miles in my living room.

Molly put cool compresses on my forehead and gave me red raspberry tea to relax my uterus.

I looked at my mother and I said, "You did this for me . . . thank you.

You did this three times? You were crazy."

She said, "No, I wasn't crazy, I was unconscious."

Then Dr. DuGre arrived and I was so happy to see him. *(She rushes over to him.)*

He checked me and he saw I was dilated . . . eight centimeters.

He said, "That is great progress for your first baby. Keep going."

Then he went into the kitchen and made himself a tuna salad sandwich.

He's flirting with my mother and then he went into the living room and he lay down and took a nap.

sherry glaser ▪

But eight centimeters means I'm in transition.
That means that the baby's head is coming through my
pelvis.
(She grimaces in pain.)
Geraldine . . . come here.
I changed my mind. I don't want to have a baby.
She said, "Okay, let's go sit on the birthing chair, that will
make it easier."
So she took me into the bathroom and sat me down on
the toilet.
There was a ten-penny nail sticking out of the wall where
Miguel and I hung our towels.
I grabbed it and I bent it.
Oooh wellll!
I realized at this time why women die in childbirth.
It's preferable.

And I had compassion for all my sisters who wanted
drugs.
But I knew whatever drug I would take would go right
through the placenta and into the baby.
I didn't want my baby on drugs so soon.
"Geraldine, I really can't take this."
She said, "If you can't take the pain, just leave your body."
I said, "Okay, bye."

I went to this place. It was right at the center of the pain
and I saw light.
Somebody touched my knee.
It was Miguel.
He said, "I love you, Kahari."
I said, "You son of a bitch, look what you did to me."
I went back to my place and I prayed to my baby.
"Baby, please . . . come down. We want to see you. Don't
you want to see us?

family secrets

Come on, I'll give you fifty dollars, right now."

Geraldine came in. She said, "I need to check you."

She reached in and she said, "I can feel the head. Would you like to feel your baby's head?"

"Yes, I would."

I reached into my body *(she does)* and I touched my baby's head.

That gave me strength.

She said, "Okay, now, your waters are still intact. Let's imagine them bursting.

Let's imagine rivers and fountains and rain coming down."

And she pinched the sack and *pssssssshhhhhhhh.*

I felt relief, for about four seconds.

And then came the pain.

It felt like Godzilla had to take a poop.

She said, "Okay, labor's over. Where would you like to deliver?"

"You mean I gotta get up?"

"Yes, and I want you to hula."

"Hula?" (She mouths . . . Fuck you.)

But I got up and I hulaed my way into the bedroom.

Oh welll . . . ohhhh. Well. Oooooohhhh welll.

And I was struck with this unbelievable urge to push.

I got on all fours like they showed us in class *(gets on the bed)*

and *ggrgrgrgrgrgghhaaaaaa.*

And nothing came out.

I didn't like that position anyway.

I got up. *(She does.)*

Miguel got behind me, he's holding me up by my armpits.

"I gotta push."

Ggrgrgrggrgggghaaaaa.

"Shit, this isn't working."

"Yes it is," they said, "we can see the head."

Everybody in the room could see the head except me.

So the doctor and the midwife took olive oil and put it on their fingers so they could stretch the perineum and they wouldn't have to give me an episiotomy. Well, they got their fingers in there, and the baby's head is in there, and I don't want anybody in there. *(She pushes them out of the way.)*

Watch out, I gotta push.

Unnngggggrrrhaaa.

Get out!

Unnnnngngngngrhaa. *(She pushes out the baby and falls back on the bed.)*

And out came this slimy blue and green thing.

And it was the most beautiful slimy thing I ever saw.

I had a baby.

And Miguel's tears were falling down on me.

And they put her right on my chest and she was whole and beautiful and she was still attached to the cord so she could get used to her new environment.

Then they cleared her throat and she took her first breath.

And you know something, I didn't love her right away.

I just felt relieved that we were done. *(She rises.)*

And of course I grew to love this baby like I have never loved anybody in my life and sometimes it's so much, that I can't bear it.

I'm afraid that something might happen to her.

In fact when she was about a week old, she had this little cough. I got so scared because you don't think your baby's sick, you think it's gonna die.

I called my mother right away.

"Ma, something's wrong with the baby. She's coughing and I'm afraid she might die."
She said, "No, Fern. Babies do that. She's just clearing her lungs, honey.
She's not going to die.
No, you're not going to get off that easy.
You're going to have to raise that baby.
Diapers and teething and toilet training. Chicken pox, elementary school and then one day,
she's gonna go to high school. You remember high school? Don't you, Fern?"
"Oh, I'm sorry, Ma. I'm really sorry."
She said, "That's okay. Remember what I said to you when you were in high school?
I wish you one just like you."
I think I got her too.

(She runs off.)

I'm coming baby, Mama's coming.
Okay, you can have a little more titty and that's it.
Why? Because, you are three years old and it's enough.
And your room is a mess.
Who is gonna clean it up?
Me.

I met a lot of people after the show and the most interesting reactions were to the birth scene. Women who have had babies already (from twenty-two to eighty-two) are bittersweetly reminded of the pain and glory of the event. Those who haven't given birth are now thoroughly terrified of the prospect. But to me the experience of that kind of pain and mastering it, learning it, surrendering to it, gave me the confidence in my body and spirit to confront the daunting task of actually raising this

sherry glaser

person that Gregory and I had created. I was the Goddess in labor. Nothing mattered, I was completely unselfconscious, pure strength and power. I was convinced during the journey of labor that the creator of the world and the universe was female.

So there she was, Dana Lynn, a girl. Of course I had said, whatever I get I'll be happy with, just five fingers and toes, but secretly I wanted a girl. So I could give her all the dreams and love and ideas I never got. She was immediately beautiful to me. The moment of birth is exhilarating. The sound of the baby gushing forth *flloooopppp*. It's a glorious mess and the smell . . . it's the darkest, sweetest odor. It's blood and molasses and soil and mystery and the relief is unparalleled. They put her right in my arms and she was blue and green and she wasn't breathing. I got scared. They were asking, "What's her name?" I said, "Dana." They called to her, "Hello, Dana, Hi, Dana, you're with us now, come on." They jostled her gently and cleared her throat and she took her first breath. A tiny yelp came from her, a baby bird, and she took my nipple almost immediately. The room seemed full of spirits and fairies and people who loved me. I'd never seen Gregory cry before. He watched his child come from his lover and he would never be the same.

They weighed her on a hanging scale; seven pounds, ten ounces. They wiped the vernix from her face and eyes (my mother and I wiped it on our hands and face) and swaddled her in a cotton blanket. Everyone held her. But Gregory, he merged with her. He was the father.

My mother called up to my father, who was anxiously pacing on the balcony next door. He had heard the grunts and the screams and then the remarkably pregnant silence that followed. He came into the living room and held his granddaughter and he cried too.

My father went back to Carmel the next day, but my mother stayed with us for a week. She cooked and cleaned and shopped and bought us luxuries, like dish towels and silverware and a huge stew pot. She made chicken soup and rocked her grand-daughter a lot. We were grateful, but living together in our small bungalow was unnerving at times. She went home with six rolls of photographs and we buried the placenta in the backyard by a towering eucalyptus. Some cultures actually fry the placenta in a pan with some butter and garlic and eat it. Well, it fed the baby for nine months, what could be so bad? But we buried it nonetheless. Back to the mother.

It was cold in December, not freezing, but the air was crisp and Gregory wanted his girls warm and cozy. He moved the bedding into the living room, right next to the wall heater, and we camped there for the next few weeks. We were high on baby fumes. The first few weeks we couldn't get over the fact that we had created such an extraordinary light in the world. She slept between us, so it was easy to nurse her on demand; I just rolled over and plopped it in. She ate to her heart's content. Gregory would lie with her in the morning while I tried to get my body back together. He would stare into her eyes for hours and she back at him. They were in bliss.

I, however, was in agony. Not all the time, but I couldn't have a bowel movement. I was naturally sore from the delivery, but I had scared myself out of having a shit. I didn't want to tear any-thing already painfully sensitive, so I basically held it in. On the fifth day nature demanded her way and I had to go. Well, it was a monstrous movement and I popped a huge vein, which be-came a hemorrhoid the size of my fist. The next few months would be daily suffering on the toilet. I was in great pain. Greg-ory would sit with me and hold my hand and kiss my forehead and tell me he loved me while I cried. I felt ugly and crippled and embarrassed and I never felt so loved in my whole life.

So the first few months of Dana's life was full of great lessons for me. Not always fun. Greg was intimate with her, spending all his time talking to her and cooing her and biting her up. I found myself in a heightened state of jealousy. I wanted that attention.

One morning I was completely ignoring them both and planning my divorce, when he asked me what the matter was. I said, "Why should you care? All you care about is Dana." He laughed. I screamed, "I want that attention. I want you to love me like that." It hit me like a lightning bolt. "I never got that from my father. He never had time to look at me like that and love me like that. He had to go to work." I was bawling my eyes out. "I never had it, and I want it now. I want my daddy." I fell in a heap on the living room carpet. I cried for an hour and it was over. Then I felt the relief of uncovering such a poisonous sentiment. I was so happy that Dana had this ever present, vital and powerful guardian. My hemorrhoid started to heal and we got on with our family.

Dana was six months old when we left San Diego. Even with wonderful reviews and a solid following I couldn't get a booking in a regular theater. It was time to go. We sold our old car, packed up our boxes (which would become a too frequent event from then on) sent them UPS to my mother's house, and got a plane to Monterey.

It wasn't fun living at my mother's house. Well, sometimes it was fun. I liked that the three generations of females could spend time together. But the tension between my husband and father was palpable. My father just didn't like Greg. He thought he should get a job, but at the time Gregory was convinced that his fortune lay in guessing which football, baseball, or basketball team would win that day. He was a gambler.

I never had been interested in watching sports. My father watched them, but I thought they were boring. Gregory introduced me to the beauty, the poetry, the grace of pro sports. He said that it was the only form of entertainment in which you really didn't know what was going to happen at the end. Anything could; someone could even die. I joined him on Sundays to watch the magnificent prowess of these men, their agility, their balance, their strength, their asses. Football players have the best asses.

But on the days Greg had a bet on the game, it wasn't fun anymore. His anger at the referees or the sometimes human errors of the players was way out of proportion; sometimes he would be on the verge of tears if someone missed a field goal. He would spend hours poring over the sports stats, comparing performances and percentages, trying to calculate which team was due a win or could at least cover the point spread. He saw it as a science. I saw it as fifty-fifty, no matter what the professionals said.

Greg's track record was actually pretty good. He did pay the rent a couple of times with his winnings and he always shared them with me. That's what made it unusual; he was generous and up-front about it. He thought it could really be a way of life. With his ever-so-charming personality, he convinced my father to back his venture with a thousand dollars. I hated it. Every game had Greg's self-esteem riding on it as well as the approval of my father, not to mention his financial investment. He played with the money; it went up and down, but no big profits were seen.

Then came the Tyson fight. Greg picked Tyson to win. He called it a "lock pick" meaning that it was a sure thing and he not only wanted my father to back him, but my rich uncle as well. They refused. They would be watching the fight at my dad's house and they really didn't want to worry about money, they just wanted to enjoy the sport. How anyone could actually enjoy watching two men beat the shit out of each other is and will always be beyond my concept of entertainment. I think it goes back to some sort of caveman behavior. It was a historic fight. I think it lasted forty-eight seconds. Mike KOed this guy as easily as he would have knocked me out. The party was over and Greg was fuming. He couldn't understand why my father had hesitated to "invest." He vowed he would show my dad and Uncle Paul and everyone else he was a genius at this.

Meanwhile, I had secured a performance space at the Grovemont Theater in Monterey. I had won the Monterey Bay Critics award the year before for *Coping* and the theater was glad to have me back. It was a chance for some money. I was pretty shaky. I hadn't been on the stage since Dana was born, but the time had come.

I used some old monologues, definitely improved upon with new writing, and changes that Greg had suggested. Miguel did tarot readings for the audience and I had a Japanese character named Daniel who liked to gamble and be a househusband, taking care of his baby while his wife worked outside the home. And there was Paulette, a Billie Holiday type who thought every malady she suffered could possibly be cancer. I also had a birth scene. I had written a rough outline of the monologue, but I basically just told it like it was. Part of the magic included bringing Dana out with me to begin the monologue and nursing her right there in front of the audience. I wanted to make nursing the most natural thing in the world to witness, because it was the most natural thing in the world to do.

But in the back of my mind I worried that maybe this show business career wasn't going to happen after all, that maybe I just should give up and get a real job. I voiced my feelings to Greg on the way to the theater.

He said, "Honey, you never know what might happen. You never know who might be in the audience." He was a prophet. That night a bright, blue-eyed, compact man with fuzzy brown hair came up to me after the performance. His name was Harry Winer. He said he was a director from Warner Brothers and he thought I was extremely talented. He was moved and completely entertained by my work. He gave me his card and told

family secrets

me he would help me. He would be in touch. I had heard this before, but he was genuine. There was hope.

The Grovemont run was limited and I needed to work. I wanted to get out of my parents' house, maybe go to San Francisco, like Whoopi did. Follow her footsteps. We didn't make it to San Francisco.

We went to Santa Cruz, where we found a gallery/performance space. It would cost twenty-five dollars a night and we were responsible for lights, sound, tickets, props. It was a modest space; you could fit a hundred chairs if you wanted to; we averaged about seventy-five dollars a night. We had no money for advertising and relied on free listings and word of mouth. The extraordinary attribute of this place was hidden behind the black curtain that backdropped the stage. It was a life-size wax replica of the Last Supper. Jesus and all his pals were behind me every night, but how could we not take advantage of such an opportunity? We wrote Miguel's signature piece.

Seems Miguel was struggling. He had found the New Age but could not quite "manifest" his fortunes in real terms. His heart was pure and he found joy in a blade of grass. His enthusiasm was as delightful as a dog going on a walk and, in fact, dogs were his greatest teachers.

"You know when you come home your dog is like 'Hey!! You're home!' He wags his tail all over the stage. When was the last time your lover did that?"

He was married to Kahari, but he was having trouble with his father-in-law because he couldn't find himself a decent job. In fact the only job he could find was that of a waiter. Frustrated and humiliated, he turned to a past-life therapist. She told him:

"Miguel, the trouble is, you have been a waiter in every one of your past lives. In fact in your first incarnation, you were the waiter at the Last Supper. The only way for you to get off the Karmic wheel is to go back through hypnosis and heal that life-

sherry glaser ■

time." He agreed. He then pulled back the curtain and there they were, Jesus and the boys. The audience fell off their chairs.

All was going well. Harry did call and said he would be setting up a showcase for me soon. He was in the middle of a film, but he was thinking of me. I was excited.

We were sitting downstairs in our apartment. I was nursing Dana, as usual, and Greg was writing. The phone rang. It was my mother from upstairs. She wanted to talk to us. We trundled up the stairs with Dana. We sat down on the couch. My father turned off the TV. This must be serious—that TV was always on, no matter what. My mother said, "We just got a call from Uncle Paul. He said that Greg called and asked if he could borrow three thousand dollars because of a bet he lost."

I laughed, holding the baby in my arms. "That's ridiculous! Why would he say that? That's crazy, honey, isn't it?" Greg didn't look up.

"Oh no," I said, "what happened?" Greg explained that he had bet on the Oakland A's to win the pennant. He was sure it was a "lock pick" and he wanted us to get out of our hole, so he bet money we didn't have, and then Kirk Gibson hit a home run in the ninth inning of the second game and it turned the Dodgers around. They won. I was in shock. Actually, shock is a mild word to describe what I was feeling. I wanted to decapitate him. How dared he call my uncle and ask him? How dared he bet that kind of money . . . how dared he not tell me? I felt like a fool. I was humiliated. I was devastated. I wanted a divorce.

I hadn't been paying attention to the attention he was paying to the games while I worked at the Santa Cruz Art league. I had trusted him. I didn't think we could get over this and I was scared. He owed the money to his bookie. This hobby had become a threat. My parents refused to pay the debt and I didn't blame them. Gregory would have to find his way out of this deep, dark hole. We finally went downstairs to have this out. I was in such a frenzy, yelling and crying, that I don't know how

family secrets

I got from one end of the room to the other. I was emotional lightning burning everything in my path, and Greg was singed for weeks.

Greg scrambled to find the money and ended up borrowing money from his brother and a friend of his and paid off the bookie. I wanted him to go into therapy, something he despised. He said no one could tell him anything about himself he didn't already know, but I wouldn't stay with him unless he went. He did go once or twice and he stopped betting. He realized he couldn't make a living at it. He had to find a real career, something that fed his soul and would contribute to the world and make some money.

We also had to move out. The convenience of staying with my parents now meant having to face my father's inquisitions every night and my parents lack of faith in my marriage and my husband. We had to go. A friend at the time told me she thought Greg was the obstacle that kept me from realizing my full potential. He was the reason I had been struggling so long, and if I'd rid myself of him, my career would skyrocket. I started to believe her. But here I was with a baby and a shaky career and no home and there was something important between Greg and me. I couldn't define it at the time, but when he kissed me or there was tenderness between us or he made me laugh, so simply and innocently, the gambling wound started to heal. I wouldn't let him go.

We ended up subletting a cabin on Laurels Grade. The sliding glass doors looked over the mountains and the Salinas Valley. It was there that Dana had her first birthday and took her first steps. We were listening to Garrison Keillor on the radio one afternoon. She had been balancing really well for a while and this day she let go of my hands, turned, and took three steps away from me. She turned back and said, "Bye-bye." I cried. My baby was growing up.

I was working at my desk one afternoon when I got a call

from Monica. We hadn't spoken much because of the terrible hurt still lodged between us, but she needed to talk. She had had a ménage à trois with her chiropractor and his assistant and James found out. They were on the ropes. It looked like they were getting a divorce. I wondered if this was a sign. Perhaps, since her relationship wasn't working out, we were meant to be together. As Monica told me the erotic and sordid details of the betrayal, I realized that even with her broken marriage and Greg's gambling, the petty fights we habitually manufactured, I wanted to be with this man.

More wonderful things were happening to my career. Some big shots from Island Pictures had come to see my show. They were young and hip, they had money and power, and they were very enthusiastic about my work. They had driven all the way up from L.A. to Santa Cruz in a limo. I was impressed. They said they were too. I didn't think I did a very good show that night, because the audience was audible, but these guys could see through the rough edges into the potential. The stove was on and we were cookin' on two burners.

Harry called again; he had arranged to showcase me at the Cort Theater. We were very excited. There were agents from CAA, people from Warner Brothers, people who could write you a check on the spot. I was frozen fear, a fearcicle. These were the big players and they were all going to be looking at me, wanting something from me. As far as I knew I didn't have much to offer them and they might all be polite at the end of the show because they were friends with Harry, but they would all tell me to go home and play. But they didn't. They stood up at the end and shouted bravo. When I saw Greg at the end of the show, he was beaming. He held me and said, "You're gonna be a star." Harry said it was like Christmas. Everybody was buzzing with excitement. As they say in Hollywood, the heat was on.

That night I was signed by a young agent at CAA and I got an offer from Warner Brothers to write a sitcom. I had arrived.

The WB studio wanted me to write a sitcom based on the character of Grandma Rose. The option that they presented me with provided that I would get ten thousand dollars. Five thousand up front and the rest in a month or sixty days to maintain the option. We were rich. We went to Santa Cruz and bought a 1987 Saab Turbo, a used Saab. My father warned us against that purchase. And he said if we insisted on the vehicle to definitely have it checked out by a good mechanic before signing the lease. We thought he was being overprotective and controlling.

A few days later we were to drive down to L.A. to do another showcase, this time at the Tiffany Theater on Sunset Boulevard. Moving up in the world. We packed up the Saab and the little one and drove down the 101. After we got the first of many speeding tickets, we stopped to fill up the car and clean the windows. Gregory went to turn the car and leave the filling station and . . . nothing. No spark, no murmur, just the hum of the fan. We tried to get it going for about ten minutes before it started. We realized after the process duplicated itself two or three more times that after a long drive our Saab had to rest. Our car was a prima donna.

The showcase went well. More agents, more celebs. It was time to move to L.A. Greg found us an old converted barn in Topanga. It was on a canyon and our neighbors were warm and wonderful and all was good in our immediate world. I went to work writing at the studio with a fabulous young writer, Wendy Goldman, who shepherded me through the Valley of the Studio. The only problem was the car. I had been driving along the winding canyon road when the oil light went on. I didn't stop immediately, unaware of the mortal danger to the heart of the engine. I had fried the rings.

After all was said and done it cost over four thousand dollars, not including the cost of the car we had to rent and use while we waited three months to get the parts the mechanic needed. Gregory wanted to drive it off a cliff. We couldn't sell it, we didn't own it. We couldn't even scrap it for junk. You need the pink slip for that.

One dark night Greg took the license plates off and had it towed up the hill, right to the road and left it there. We hoped they would tow it away and we'd never see it again, but we left the hull number on and of course that number is on the registration, and while in fact they did tow it, they sent an ominous, official-looking document which instructed us that they had impounded the car and that cost seventy-five dollars; it cost seventy-five dollars a day to keep it there. We ignored the note and hoped they would make the car into a nice planter. We bought a Honda.

I made the last payment on the Saab in December of '94. I hadn't seen the car in three years. All in all, it cost about eighteen thousand dollars. I had the pink slip, the certificate of ownership, framed and sent it to my father.

I would drive to the Warner Brothers studio every morning and work in Wendy Goldman's office. I loved Wendy. She was funny and easy to write with. She had her own office and her own secretary, named Phil. We had come up with a pitch and a show for Rose. I thought that would be pretty easy. Just put her in a family that resembled mine and give her all the great story lines of my life. When we went to the head of the department with my grand idea, he shot it down with a loaded gefilte fish. "Too Jewish. We don't want her in a Jewish family. We need contrast. Come up with some character that contrasts with hers." Here I had this little old Jewish lady with no family. She was a little old orphan.

Wendy and I tried to team her up with a young black jazz saxophonist. "No," they said. "Rose has got to be the hip one." Okay. We hooked her up with a young, white genetic scientist with kooky lab assistants. "No, there aren't enough story lines in a lab." Our last and final attempt was to pair her up as a roommate with a young white-bread journalist from Boston. "Not

family secrets

dramatic enough." My contract was up. I kissed Wendy goodbye and got in my car and drove to the mall. I called my mother.

"Mom, I'm so confused. I'm getting anti-Semitism from Jews. I don't know what to do." She couldn't understand it either.

It's odd, because all the gentile and pagan people who come to be in my audience make a point of telling me, "Listen, I'm not Jewish, but I loved the show. It's so universal and touching."

I say, "Yeah, it's about family. And we all can relate to that." The only people who complain about the ethnicity of my show are the Jewish executives in show business who are ashamed or trying to play down their own cultural background.

In fact, I wasn't Jewish anymore. My belief in God had changed a long time ago. I never really identified with the Jewish religion at all. I went to temple on holidays so I wouldn't have to go to school. I fasted on Yom Kippur so I could lose a pound or two. No one ever really explained the religion part to me. Gregory was more familiar with the history of the Jews than I was. He had read the Old Testament. To my father it was more political than anything. The survival of Israel was paramount to him and he'd defend the homeland till the bitter end. It's the identification with six million that keeps him and many like him devoted to the worthy cause of being Jewish.

I'm not ashamed or trying to avoid the cultural Jew that I am, but I believe in the Mother, not the Father. I find it offensive that the God of the Jews was jealous and vengeful and that women are all but absent from the first Testament. It says that Abraham begat and Jacob begat and I'll tell you in all my days I've never seen a man beget anything. Women beget and I want that on the record.

The Cosmic Mother, The White Goddess. When God was a Woman. All based on hard archaeological evidence that the first evidence of worship was associated with female God, the Goddess. It just makes sense. Here they are, the humans, newly erect on the planet and everything must seem like a miracle, but particularly birth and death. And since the realm of birth was ruled by the woman, the natural association was that all life originally came from her. I find it hard to fathom that people actually believed that Eve came from Adam, from his rib yet. This information, to me, is just an example of the systematic pirating of woman's natural power into Judeo-Christian beliefs that actually began the violent destruction of peaceful creative matriarchal communities.

The beginnings of language emerged from the female because of the nature of her responsibilities. The men had to go out and hunt, which was a mostly silent experience in order not to scare away the animals. The women, however, sat around the fire, minding and educating the children. When the young ones would wander too close to the fire a sound of warning would spring forth, *Ayyyahannnooo!!!!* The women agreed that this was a fine way to remind the children to be careful of the fire. They used it over and over. Language was born.

They were also the first doctors, because they were in charge of gathering. They had to determine what this cornucopia of flora was all about, what was for seasoning, what was for bathing, what was poison (many gave their lives for this generous discovery), and what was for curing that nasty pustule on Oona's back. They shared their findings of pharmacopeia through language.

So I am spiritually committed to the Goddess and Mother Earth, but in my blood and on my face, and in my culture and where I grew up and with whom, and the fact that when I hear klezmer music I have to dance or cry, I will always be a Jew.

So there I was, back to Lobby L. The bottom floor. We were stunned and couldn't figure out how this had happened. I couldn't get my agent to return my calls. I had to get a job. I had to find a theater. If I thought it was difficult to find a theater in San Diego, how would I find one in the place where all the transitory species of actors migrated.

family secrets

I opened the Yellow Pages and looked under "Theater." I called about fifty of them from the Doolittle to the Tiffany. Nobody would take a chance. So I rented a theater in Venice all by myself. The Rose. I thought that was a good omen. There were about fifty seats, folding chairs, really. A young guy who drove a motorcycle did the lights.

Harry had told me that the show needed a through line. The characters were brilliant, the writing as well, but if I could tie it all together it would be a tremendous package. I was already doing my mother and grandmother and had a decent monologue for my father, so the theme seemed obvious. The title came while I was driving down the 101 freeway—*Family Secrets*.

I asked Robyn from Hot Flashes to direct. Why? Well, she was living in L.A., I needed an outside eye, and even though Gregory had been working on the show with me for years, I wouldn't . . . I couldn't allow him to direct the show. I wasn't ready to give up that much power; he was my husband. So if he became the director he would have much more power over me and I couldn't handle that, not yet. I hired Robyn and ended up paying for that for the next four years, because when I finally fired her I felt so guilty that I actually gave her a piece of the show. And somehow she multiplied it through the years into probably millions of dollars. I'm still paying her.

I could have the Rose on Sunday nights; that was it. We advertised in the free press and got an average of ten to fifteen people each week and we ate a lot of oatmeal. Until Barbara Esanston came. She was a talk radio psychologist, and talk she did. She got on the radio and told everyone that they must see the show. It was the most hilarious, most moving thing she had ever seen. Gregory and I were sitting in our Topanga barn listening to her report on the radio. We were doing little jigs around the brick floor. Then she gave the phone number for reservations and our phone started to ring. We were the box office. We sold out for the next three weeks and then the owner of the theater, noticing our success, offered us the whole week. We were in business. Suddenly the newspapers were interested and were setting up reservations. We were touching the hem of nirvana once again.

I won the *Los Angeles Times* Outer Critic Circle award for Solo Performance as well as the *L.A. Weekly*'s Award. During my acceptance speech of the *L.A. Weekly*'s plaque I thanked my producers, my agent, my mother, my director, my daughter, and my husband, but most of all I thanked myself. For the first time in my career I publicly acknowledged my own contributions, my talent, my hard work in creating and presenting my work. It was exhilarating and terrifying, because once I claimed it somehow it meant I was responsible for doing it and living up to its expectations and beyond. But I took that risk. And then I got sick.

I wasn't feeling real good. I didn't make a big deal out of it, because one of the problems was I was losing weight and to an ex-bulimic that's not the worst thing that can happen. But then I was experiencing pain. There was a sharp stabbing pain in my liver, the gall bladder area, and I was losing weight rapidly. The *L.A. Times* was the first newspaper to report my illness. I had just been reviewed and the critics mentioned the physical impact of the illness. "Waiflike," "Ghostly in appearance," "Wan."

Now if you've seen me lately, I'm anything but waiflike. I'm solid, solid as a boulder. I had to go to the doctor. Not the chiropractor, not the homeopath, though I tried them first without success. I went to a female doctor in Venice expecting the worst. I mean with my history I was a prime candidate for AIDS and, of course, my old, familiar fear, cancer.

I had her examine me from head to toe, inside and outside. I would have to wait three days for the results of the tests. I called on the appointed third day. I didn't have AIDS. I didn't have cancer. I had a Giardia. "What?"

"It's an intestinal parasite. You'll have to take an antibiotic to kill it and you'll be fine."

"A parasite!" I was thrilled. I ran around telling everyone. "I've got a parasite! I'm so happy. I've got a parasite." It was one of the happiest days of my life. But I was puzzled. Where on earth did I come up with that one? You get them from drinking water where the parasite lives, like a mountain stream . . . oh yeah.

About nine months before that, we had gone to Greg's brother's wedding in Colorado. I remembered one afternoon I went for a walk all by myself up the Rockies. I saw a little brook. I was thirsty. I bent down to refresh myself and took a long drink. Two guys came by on a snowmobile and called out, "Hey, lady, don't drink that water. It's not clean."

I thought, "Jeez, what do they know. These are the Rocky Mountains, for God's sake."

One of the drawbacks of taking the medication was having to stop breast-feeding. I was really disappointed at the thought. I wanted Dana to have the choice to wean herself, but she was two years old and I thought she would survive the trauma. I took her out into our field behind our house and explained that she could have no more titty because mommy was sick and needed to take medicine that would come through the milk and wouldn't be good for her. I cried more than she did.

But after I had killed the nasty little stowaway and my body cleared out the remnants of the chemical toxins of the medicine she asked me if she could resume having her milk. I wasn't sure if it had dried up, but sure enough, a little tug and a suck and she was supping at my breast once again.

Sometimes my life got way ahead of me. I didn't see it coming, or I didn't want to see it. But our marriage was flushing itself down the toilet. Although Greg had volunteered to stay home and take care of Dana, it wasn't good for him. He wasn't getting enough social interaction with adults, so he would occupy his free time with beer and pot and TV and became very unhappy. We fought all the time. He was insinuating that I had dissuaded him from law school, because if it hadn't been for me . . . I was resentful, because I would go off to work and be making the money and I would come home and the house would be a mess and there was nothing cooked and I still had to put Dana to bed.

I would do all the shopping. And he would do the laundry and cooking, but he wasn't enthusiastic about it, so nothing was done with pride and a feeling of accomplishment. So he was miserable and if I confronted him on anything we would fight. It got so our house in Topanga had no doors on their hinges anymore because I would slam them so hard. In fact, one time I slammed a door and it didn't break off the hinge, so I slammed it again and it did. He wanted to work on the show and I wouldn't let him. He tried to get a job—well, he didn't try that hard, but he didn't have much luck anyway, being a waiter is a premium position in L.A. and he didn't have the stamina to beat the competition. He did try. And he started to write. I knew he was a writer.

One night we stumbled upon some affection still gasping between us. We made love by the fire of our potbellied stove. Since it had been so long since we'd been sexual, I had no idea where I was in my cycle. We were right on time. We were separated when I found out I was pregnant. He had gone to San Diego to stay with friends. I was pretty sure the marriage wouldn't last much longer and we could barely support one child, let alone two . . . not to mention the cost of simply giving birth. I decided to have an abortion. I didn't give Greg much of a choice. It was my body, my life, and I would make the decision. I went to my parents' house in Carmel and had the procedure done in Monterey. My mother went with me for support.

I will defend a woman's right to an abortion to the end, but it is not a good decision for me. I mourned that loss. I still do. I feel furious that my grief and my personal decision should be scrutinized by anyone but myself. It is my business, my body, and my pain and I am the authority and the judge, no one else. The zeal of the antiabortion fanatics makes it nearly impossible for a woman dealing with such a horrendous decision to mourn and heal the loss. But I do.

After the procedure my mother and I went back to the house and spent a very quiet evening. I sat with my father and he held me and I cried a lot. I couldn't explain to Dana; she was only three. It seemed too complicated for her little psyche. She knew something on some level, but I only told her that I was very sad and I had felt sick. I will explain to her one day soon. I had one day to recuperate and then I had to return to L.A. and go to work. Dana stayed with my mother and my father came with me to help me survive the reentry.

The theater seemed very dark that night. It was about three quarters full, but I was in pain and shock. I hadn't told anybody about my weekend, but I don't exactly have a poker face. My producers were concerned, but I wasn't going to reveal anything. I did the show. Having to become Kahari and go through the experience of childbirth after such a loss was devastating. At the same time, reliving the birth and simulating the experiences over time was a poultice to the wound. But that night was excruciating.

It wasn't only Kahari that I suffered through but Rose as well. She is the embodiment of my love story with Greg. While he was drowning himself in tequila on the Mexican border and our marriage was as lively as the worm at the bottom of his shot glass, I was speaking of how we had fallen in love, the passion of our sex life, and the eternity of our love. I was a mess.

In April, with the help of Bunny and some good counseling, Gregory and I reconciled. I got a job in San Francisco at the Improv. Good money and a free place to live. Part of our reconciliation was about my acknowledging Greg as a creative partner. We had to strike a balance of power in our relationship and it was then he finally got recognition for all the patient hours and days and months of work he had contributed to the show. The program now read "Written by Sherry Glaser and Gregory Howells." It made a huge difference in our lives.

It had been difficult for me to see the amount of writing he had done on the show because it was subtle. "Change this line to that" or, "If you say it in this order it will be funnier." He has a natural sense of theater, of timing, of comedy, and he shared these gifts with me generously. His jokes were brilliant, but I hardly gave him any credit. I was so worried about my own worth I couldn't let him in on the project we had spent so much of our lives together feeding and nurturing as consistently as our own child. Dana was also blossoming from the consistent love she got; plentiful breast milk was still available to her when she was three and a half.

So we bopped up to San Francisco. We had a great little apartment up the street from the Improv. Major city, great opening night. At least I thought so. I opened the *Chronicle* the next day as casually as I would butter my bagel that morning, expecting the best. Oops. There it was. My first scathing review. The reviewer hated it. A bomb had exploded in my ego and I lay in pieces all over our Nob Hill flat. I saw the review was a personal attack. How could it not be? I am the show. The critic was outraged, disgusted, and offended by my work and I had to perform that night with those very specific phrases dancing in my head.

Everyone at the club told me what an asshole this guy was. He only liked musicals and productions with bouncy, flouncy blondes. Still, my performance that night was affected. Every word was tentative, every gesture unsure, every idea embarrassed. I was in crisis. I called a local psychic for a healing. She came to the apartment the next day.

"So, how big was the review?"

"Full page."

"Full page, huh? And was there a picture?"

"Yes, two pictures."

"Uh-huh, and was it really bad?"

"Yes, it was."

"He didn't say it was mediocre?"

"No, he hated it."

"The man took a whole page in a major American newspaper and talked about you the whole time and used two pictures. I think it's wonderful. Congratulations." The words bounced off the wall and tried to get into my head.

"How can you say it's fantastic?"

"You affected him so deeply he couldn't contain his feelings. It's scandalous. As long as it wasn't middle of the road and he was passionate in his hatred for it, then it's great. People love a scandal. They'll want to come and see what all the fuss is about." I got back on the horse and rode.

It wasn't the last bad review I got. In Florida a female reviewer (Jewish as well) hated the show and dissected it with a vicious pen. There was a huge picture and a full-page article. Her biggest complaints were that it had a lot of "potty humor" and was "too Jewish." We sold out, extended the show there, and I won the Southern Florida Award for Best Actress in Comedy.

"Too Jewish." I've heard that little anti-Semitic phrase from more Jews than I'd like to share a pork roast with.

It was in San Francisco that I discovered the show's magic ingredients. I started working with Art Wolfe, an experienced director of both TV and stage, including Penn and Teller, the comedic geniuses of magic. We were rehearsing at the Second Stage theater across the street from the Improv, where I was supposed to move if the show was a success, when we started to discuss the transitions between characters. I'd been doing costume and character changes backstage while there were slides and music entertaining the audience in the interim. He said that every-

sherry glaser ☒

body doing a one-person show left the stage to make changes. He wanted magic.

He told me that Penn and Teller did a piece with cups and balls. The beauty of the trick was that they painstakingly demonstrated the illusion to the audience before they executed it, but despite the explanation, the audience still couldn't figure out how it was done, even though it was done right before their eyes. "That's what I want," he said.

I said, "Okay. What if I transform right in front of their eyes? Instantly." The most difficult part of the trick was not the transformation but my physical exposure to the audience. I still had problems with my body image, and for a long moment I would be standing in only my clinging Lycra unitard. After all my work and success as a writer, actress, wife, and mother, I was still bound by the shackles of culturally defined beauty and the addiction to the unthreatening form of a shapeless girl. How my body was perceived for those thirty seconds became the focus of an otherwise brilliant discovery. I was ready for the confrontation with myself.

We came up with a two-way mirror on the vanity where I sat to put on my wigs and touches of make-up. It worked so beautifully. Over the next month or two, with each unveiling, I learned to love and accept my curves and generous shape. Greg inspired me. "Sherry, you're not a little girl anymore, you're not a teenager. You're a woman. A full-bodied, beautiful woman. You're the Goddess." It helped a lot.

Having the show at the Improv was a bit odd, because people coming there expected to see stand-up comedy. The owner of the Improv decided to bring in a late show, Rob Becker's *Defending the Caveman*. I would be the early show at eight, and he would come in at ten. The problem was my show ran until ten-five, sometimes, ten-ten. I'd have to cut twenty minutes. How was I going to do that? Each piece had been meticulously written; everything was essential. I was insulted and angry that he would even ask me to do such a thing. I was also suffering from the stigma of being the early show and Rob being the "headliner." The owner suggested I cut the intermission. I laughed. After "giving birth" I was exhausted and desperately needed the break; I could never get through the whole show without an intermission. But I had no choice. I thank him to this day for his invention.

The show became an odyssey, a ride. Metamorphosing from one character to the next was brilliant. That, with the transformations on stage, has become my signature.

The show ran in San Francisco for six months. We closed and we had no work. We retreated to a monastery, Madre Grande. We settled in a cozy trailer among the monks in the high desert of Southern California and cohabited with the coyotes and lizards and the enormous boulders that surrounded the camp, which in silhouette against the turquoise blue sky distinctly resembled a giant female lying down for a long, deep sleep. We basked in her shadow and lived communally with the monks and others who had left civilization for various reasons, some religious, some health. There was a woman there who was environmentally ill from the overwhelming pollution of the cities. She seemed odd, bathing in bleach and wearing aluminum foil to reflect the sun, but she was only one of the host of characters living on the land. It cost one hundred dollars a month to live in this splendor, so we had enough left over from the San Francisco booty to last a few months. As the money trickled down to double digits, word came from the Coconut Grove in Florida that I had a job.

There was work to be done on the show prior to the Florida debut. Florida was important since news of the show would filter up to New York because of all the "snowbirds" (New Yorkers who flew south for the winter). It was the perfect out-of-town tryout. I called Art. He had gotten a pilot to direct and I became a nuisance compared to the high rolling hills of Hollywood. Our rehearsal diminished to a one-hour phone call to completely rework the show. I fired him. Gregory was in the trailer when I told Art. He was dancing on the couch because he knew that finally I had come to the conclusion that the true director of *Family Secrets* was Greg Howells.

Gregory had had no previous experience as a director. He had something else. He had graduated from Ohio State University with a B.A. in English, but he didn't major in English as a liberal lark. It was serious and consuming for him. Literature is his passion. He bathes in Shakespeare and showers himself with Dickens. He has been trying to get me to finish *Madame Bovary* for months, calling it a perfect piece of objective literature. He is dedicated to character, story, place, and time, all the elements that make for great theater. What further elevates him as my director, besides his intimate connection with my process and life story and the actual characters, being his relations now, is his genius at writing. He has perfect pitch. He can hear the flaws in the writing and easily remedy them with phrasing or editing. And on top of all that, he is funny. Deeply, unpredictably, and seriously funny.

We were in San Diego when Gregory came up with a new beginning for the show. At the Gaslamp in San Diego, still under Art's direction, we had the facsimile of a house on stage. And to begin with, Mort entered through the front door. Greg had real problems with the set because he felt it distracted from the play, which, he said, primarily took place on my body. He thought the stage should look as if it were floating in space, mostly black. All attention should be on me, not the colonial beamed ceiling. But it was the beginning he was after. We were walking in Balboa Park, a magnificent tribute to architecture and nature, when he presented his genesis.

"It's dark. Mort is sitting in his chair, he's on the phone. We know that, but the audience doesn't. He says, 'uh-huh. . . . uh-huh. . . . uh-huh . . . yeah.' A light comes up from behind him, a blue light, just framing him. 'Uh-huh . . . Fern? . . . Fern? . . .

Can I ask you one question? Why did you write the checks when the money wasn't there?' Lights up."

I laughed. I said, "That's brilliant, but I don't think I can do it. You're asking me to sit in the dark, as a man, and the first word, not even a word really, that you want me to say is 'Uh-huh?'" We walked around the park for another hour and a half and all I said, in various tones and colors was, "Uh-huh."

I was at the Michigan Women's Music and Comedy Festival in August of '93, when I got the news that I would open Off-Broadway in New York that September. I believe all eight thousand women there heard my scream for joy. Finally.

The call is "Five minutes." Everyone on Broadway, Off Broadway, and off-off-Broadway, hears that at five minutes before the hour of 8 P.M. I find myself in the prestigious and exhilarating company of *Miss Saigon, Angels in America,* Jackie Mason, Lynn Redgrave's *Shakespeare for My Father,* Anna Deveare Smith's *Twilight, Kiss of the Spider Woman, Carousel, The Glass Menagerie.* When we walk out on that stage, no matter how big the company is or if one is all alone, it is the New York stage and it is one of the most demanding places in the world.

"Five minutes." Some people have their last cigarette, some people vocalize, some finish their coffee. In my theater, my stage manager makes the call. She draws the curtain to my space and everyone leaves the backstage area.

I sit before my altar in the dark. All my rocks and crystals are laid before me on a lavender cloth. My clay Goddess with the rose blooming from her pelvis, Quan Yin, Chinese Goddess cast in bronze. A photograph of myself in a tepee in Northern California, draped in bearskin; a greeting card with a rendition of a warrior spirit. Crystals amethysts, stones, and the whale card from my medicine deck (a deck of cards that uses animals as symbols for the soul's path. It is based on Native American teachings). The whale represents the primordial voice, the original language.

I flick on the Bic lighter to illuminate the holy altar. (I used to light a candle, but I forgot to blow it out one Sunday evening and the flame was so small that no one noticed it burning in its votive glass. It burned till Monday morning and everyone was quite perturbed that I had almost burned down the theater.) Pungent incense is burning so the smoke can carry my prayers upward: "Help me through this show tonight. I want to let go and trust this instrument, this gift, and express myself fearlessly." I grab my empty plastic Evian bottle and blow air into it. I fill my lungs to capacity and then release it at an even pace to make sort of a bassoon sound echo through the bottle. I can hear the audience filtering in and settling down for the evening. "Places," the call is, "places."

I turn on the light and put out the incense. I put on the first character's jacket and pull the curtain. My ever-faithful wardrobe supervisor and assistant waits with headphones at the top of the steps. I am almost the first character, Mort, the father. I wait in the wings, listening to the last Nat King Cole song. . . . And while he told us many things fools, and kings, this he said to me, The greatest thing you'll ever learn is just to love and be loved in return . . . The red light goes on. "Warning."

The New York reviews were stellar, the producers aglow, my director overjoyed. For me the power was intoxicating and the schedule grueling. I would spend a year and a half on that New York stage and face the challenge of doing the same show over and over, eight times a week, into eternity. I think my opening in New York had the biggest impact on my mother and father. My mother cried at rehearsals as she realized the accomplishment of her daughter. My father had his own opening night. He had bought out the theater the night after our official opening. Everyone he ever knew, back as far as junior high school, was invited, and they came. His pride was unfathomable, his joy overwhelming. At the post-theater party that he and my mother also arranged, he hugged me and whispered in my ear, "Do you know how powerful you are? How amazing you are? How you touch people? I love you so much." To hear those words from my father completely unsolicited, and entirely based on my work, my talent, and my truths revealed sent my heart skipping down Ninth Avenue.

One of Greg's most important notes came in the middle of my tenure in New York and it had to do with the comedy of the piece. The thing about making an audience laugh is that, like heroin, it's dangerously addictive. Greg hadn't seen the show for a while and he came in to give it a tune-up. He wasn't happy with what he saw. I said, "What are you talking about? The audience was laughing the whole night."

"I know," he answered, "you've given up the drama and the story for the laughs. I want you to play the silence. I want you to go for the silence."

I was stunned. I was scared. I was so dependent on the punch-lines that I merely skimmed over the story, the drama, and waited awkwardly for the hardy-har-hars. The trouble with that kind of performance is that after a while, the laughter doesn't come because one actually winds up for the punch, and when the reaction isn't there, because subconsciously the audience senses the manipulation and gives you nothing, you fall flat on your face. He was right. I played for the silence, and in my commitment to the material and not the reaction to the material, the humor exploded like land mines.

Because of the nature of doing a one-woman show, the audience and I have a unique relationship. Unlike a standard drama or comedy, there is only me and them. If they are not responding to the humor or they are yawning or distracting themselves with the program, it is in direct response to me. Some nights I rage backstage at the insensitivity of people falling asleep in the first row, actually snoring. Some put their shopping bags on the stage or worse, their feet. Some people behave as though they are simply watching TV and think I can't possibly notice their

sherry glaser

beepers going off or their animated conversation with their neighbor. But I am reminded that they paid their $37.50 and they really don't have any responsibility to me. It is my job to entertain them, make them forget where they are, and take them on a journey of imagination. Yet there have been nights, when I have been both emotionally and physically exhausted and it has been the audience with its enthusiasm and energy that has literally pulled me through the show. But you never know who'll walk through that door.

Sometimes, on a difficult night, if I stay focused and strong and there are at least a couple of people in the mood to have a good time, I can transform the audience, but the secret is not to care. Just do the job. It has been a remarkable parallel experience of wanting the mother and fearing abandonment to performing in front of an audience. Every night I bring up the deepest psychological loss of my life and lay it before strangers.

"Let them come to you. You can't care about them. This is your house," Gregory insisted. But that four-year-old still sometimes runs the house. Each time I step out on that stage I regain more solid ground. I replace some fear with strength, I become more independent of what anyone thinks of me except me.

The task of performing *Family Secrets* every night is an emotional workout. The weight of the issues is sometimes so strong that I feel my back aching with their presence. Some nights I just put on a show. Some nights I am courageous and descend into the familiar abyss.

If I allow Mort in. If I let the pressure of the financial burdens shape his posture. If his moles and masculine musk overwhelm my feminine psyche and I allow him to wallow in his incredulity and confusion at his daughter's romantic antics. If I build up his discomfort at being forced into being in the same atmosphere as his "evil" lesbian daughter, surrounded by his "normal" companions, then the climax of the piece should shatter him with shame. If I accomplish that, then when the confrontation comes

▣ family secrets

on the phone and he reluctantly but steadfastly promises his love to his daughter, I am redeemed, and the pain between my father and myself is washed clean with an aching tenderness and fades into nothing.

My mother is a whole other story. When I am on stage and I say, "I lost my mother when I was four," I am not only claiming my loss, I'm claiming my mother's loss and I would be so bold as to assume *her* mother's loss. I would say a good percentage of the audience could echo my call. I must submerge myself in unresolved mental illness. There is a strange detachment, yet a wrenching anguish that is lying just underneath the surface, under the control of the lithium. I must be aware at all times, that without lithium she could blast off. Her inappropriate laughter is the deflection from her pain.

My mother was about to go visit her mother. She had been wanting to go for very long, but her brother, who happened to be my grandmother's psychiatrist, advised against it, saying that Mama wouldn't recognize her and it would just upset them both. My grandmother died soon after that, in the mental hospital. My mother needed a sense of closure. Her mother's urn was on the top shelf of her brother's closet in Manhattan, so my mother flew back to see her.

Everyone was reluctant to have my mother go through this process. Since she had her first breakdown, everything she wants, if it's a little out in left field, is suspect, and not only to the people who love her; her own self-doubt asks her the hardest questions. But she ignored the warnings. She and her brother brought the urn down from the closet and put it on the dining-room table on top of some newspaper. My mother opened the urn and put her hands into the ashes and cried. She said, "It wasn't really ash, it was more like gravel and little pieces of her bones."

This event, a final contact with this most intimate stranger,

sherry glaser ▪ ✴

really did lead to a letting go. When Bev takes up her mother's ashes and goes through them with her fingers, there is a feeling of rage, confusion, grief, and finally release. It is a painful reunion and there is an intake of breath from the audience until they laugh and let the breath go.

My mother's journey through the nervous breakdowns and psychotropic drugs and mental institutions were part of her path to learning and confrontation. Without that radical trip, she might not have come to examine her life. She penetrated the iron curtain of the past, confronted and forgave her mother, and with that she anticipated her full recovery from manic depression.

In June of '94 my mother decided to get off lithium. She had figured out the legitimate causes of her craziness. When she told me of the incidents that destroyed her childhood, I wept. I wept for her and I wept because she was my mother and I came through her body and somehow in the biological exchange, maybe the cell memory, I experienced it too.

In the process of her healing, she had become toxic on lithium, feeling dizzy and disorientated, and had to decrease her dose. She was making extraordinary progress. Her chemicals were rebalancing. She was watching her blood levels to be sure the lithium level stayed in a normal range. She did body work. She went to law school and graduated. She took the bar four times. She never passed, but she prepared herself for it over and over. I was proud. I was impressed. I was sure the healing was complete. I was not the only one, but I was a loud voice in the cheering section, saying, "Go, Mom, go." Because if she could heal this incurable malady, it would verify my beliefs and hers that whatever ailment one was stricken with, if one confronted the source and the course of the pain, one could heal and become whole again. She was down to two capsules every other day. I was excited. My father was nervous.

Norm was completely against her coming off lithium. He

didn't think it was doing her any harm and it certainly was doing her a lot of good. He couldn't understand her longing to be without artificial restraints, her need to experience herself completely. He just didn't want to go through the whole crazy thing again. I could understand that, but I don't buy fear as a reason for not going ahead.

He said it was too much of a risk. I said, "Gee, Dad, you're gonna be fifty-nine in October and you play tennis once a week. Isn't that a risk?"

He said, "It's not the same."

I said, "Life is a risk, Dad. You could go out in the car and on the way to work get into an accident and be killed. There is no security."

My mother took her last lithium pill on the first of July. I sent her two dozen white roses and I wrote her a poem to celebrate her liberation day. She was very touched. She sounded wonderful. She sounded real. I thought I might be hearing my mother's real voice for the first time and I was happy. My father was not happy, but there was nothing he could do but keep an eye on her.

The weekend of July 17 I went away to the country with Greg and Dana and the crew from the theater. We went to a house in the Jersey woods. It was beautiful. We went for long walks in the summer rain and inhaled the rich brocade of maple and elm. We went bowling and sailing and barbecued shark and salmon and about a hundred ears of fresh picked sweet corn and everyone had a great time. When I got home I called my mother. My father answered the phone. That's strange, I thought.

"How are you?" I asked.

"Well, we're having a bit of a crisis. Mom is having an episode."

I said, "What's up?" I didn't believe him, though I could hear her interrupting him with rude comments and laughter.

"Well," he said, "we had a rough weekend with Uncle Joe. She was very confrontational."

"Dad, tell her to stop interrupting."

"Shelly, would you stop interrupting? She sent Florrie a very confrontational letter and got her very upset." That's not unusual, I thought. "And she's laughing a lot and she seems high. Steven came up yesterday and we're trying to evaluate the situation."

"Let me talk to her." I could hear her laughing in the background as she approached the phone.

"Hello, my baby."

"Hello, Mom. What's going on?" She went into an epic story of the previous few days. She had confronted Joe and his new wife. She was explaining to Joe that his first wife, Gerty, had died from anger and not a ruptured stomach. She explained to me, "Joe's a big boy. I was just telling him the truth. Sherry, I'm gonna tell the truth from now on and I'm not gonna keep my mouth shut."

I said, "What about this letter to Florrie?" She explained the letter, and while it was confrontational, I didn't think it was earth-shattering. They were things she had needed to say to her sister for a long time. I did note that there was a bit of manipulation in the letter and when I pointed that out, I noticed her turn on me for just a moment. I brushed it away, not wanting to hear it. Then she told me a ragged tale of how she had gone over to rescue her former housekeeper who had been in desperate trouble. I tried to keep her on track of the original story, but she was wandering. Nothing out of the ordinary, really; she could go on.

I said, "Let me talk to Steven." My brother came to the phone.

"Hello, sister."

"Hello, brother. Tell me."

"Well, she seems like she's manic."

"How do you mean? I want specifics."

"Well," he said, "she's very emotional and she goes to extremes. Like this morning. I was trying to make myself breakfast. I wanted to make lox, eggs, and onions, but I couldn't find the onions. She came over and asked me why I thought I couldn't find the onions. I said, 'I don't know,' and she said, 'Because you don't think it's all right to cry. Because when you were a little boy I told you not to cry and I'm so sorry.' And she started to cry and hug me, and I thought that was kind of extreme."

"Uh-huh. Does she think she's Mary?"

"No, not yet. But she's really traveling into the past-life thing. Everything is symbolic and she believes she has really important information for Florrie about her past."

"Okay, let me talk to Mom." My mother came back to the phone.

"Okay, Mom. Now I want to talk, so don't interrupt me. First I want to say that the only reason this is going on is because everyone loves you and we're very concerned about you and . . ." I hear a weird sound like air coming out of a balloon. "Mom? . . . Mom?" She's laughing. She's laughing hysterically. "Did you tell your husband what I did? Tell your husband what I did." And she hung up. I fell on the floor and cried.

Greg walked in a few minutes later with Dana. I was hysterical. "My mother's crazy. She's gone."

Greg was very calm. He said, "This is to be expected. She's come off a very powerful drug and it's going to take her some time to stabilize."

I said, "You're wrong. It's different. I can tell by her voice. She's gone."

What could I do? I was three thousand miles away. I had to do two shows the next day. I needed to take care of myself. Although I was distraught, we decided to go to the movies to distract ourselves for a couple of hours. As we walked down the four flights of stairs of our apartment to the street I tried to explain to Dana what was happening with her grandmother. It was important for me to tell her what was going down, because when I was a kid, no one explained it to me.

I said, "Grandma is acting crazy because she got off lithium and so she needs to take her medicine to get her back to normal. But she's going to be all right. I'm upset because I love her and it reminds me of other times when she got sick, and it upsets me. So what do you think about that?"

"Well," she said, "no one's perfect." I had to laugh.

We got back from the theater and I called my father. Things were escalating. My mother was irrational and becoming aggressive, yelling in everybody's face and telling them how the world really worked and you must always tell the truth, no matter what.

They were trying to convince her to go to the hospital, to take the lithium again, but she was putting up an awful fight. My father asked if I wanted to talk to her. I said, "Okay." Reluctantly. I asked her to take some lithium, but she said that if she took some she would be giving her soul away again. I found out from my brother that she was referring to the first time she gave her soul away to Hera to save her son. I said goodnight. I had to go. I had to work in the morning. I cried, but I felt that she would be all right. My father was confident that she would take the lithium and tomorrow would be better.

In the middle of the night she woke up and decided she had to save her sister Florrie, but she knew the only way that Florrie would come see her was to go to the hospital. She was also afraid that the devil was coming for her soul, so my brother and father had to absolve her from all her wrongdoings and then they took her to the hospital. She signed herself in, which is the law in California. No one can force you into a voluntary hospital, and my father didn't want her going to a state hospital in Salinas.

family secrets

To the amazement of the doctors and nurses, she got into bed and went to sleep. Manic depressives in the state that she was in do not sleep, but she did.

When she woke up in the morning, she didn't want to be there anymore. She wanted to go home and she knew she was there voluntarily so she could walk out. The doctors and the nurses and my father and brother wanted her to stay, but that didn't matter to her, so she jumped out the window (she was on the first floor) and ran away through the woods. They chased her, but even if they could catch up with her, they couldn't touch her. She informed them, that if they did try to touch her that would be assault and battery. My mother graduated from law school and she was well aware of the law.

She made her way through the woods with staff and security trailing behind her, over to Beverly Manor, a last-stop health-care facility for elderly folk who are on their way out. That is where Grandma Rose lived. My mother waltzed up the grounds and right through the front door. She then pranced into the bingo parlor and led the crones in a couple of choruses of "As Time Goes By" and "Sunrise Sunset." When she was done singing and dancing and kissing the elders, she ran out down to Pebble Beach, where she called me.

I wasn't home. I was doing my show. I was having to become my mother at that very moment and the entry into her bouncing mental ballroom was painful. The character had an eerie aura about her. I could feel the tangible pain, fear, and confusion of insanity. I needed to have solid boundaries protecting myself from my mother at that moment, and here I was becoming my nemesis. I needed to guard my psyche, but I opened it and the demons rushed in.

I called my father between shows. He told me that she had escaped from the hospital and that she was out and on her way home. Everyone was coming to the house. Lots of people who loved her, to try to convince her to go back to the hospital and take her medication. I had to hang up and get ready for the second show. I collapsed in the hallway behind my dressing room. My company manager and my stage manager were freaked out. What could they do but pray that I would put on my makeup and Mort's costume and walk out on stage? And I did. First I put moisture base all over my face, then one eye at a time was dressed in mascara. I couldn't talk to anybody without crying, but when I heard, "Places," I got up and went to the stage entrance. Then, "Stand by," and the music . . . "In the Mood." I walked out on stage and did Mort. The love he felt for his wife that night was illuminated and fathomless. But Bev was . . . astonishing. Gone was the audience and the costume and the character. It was her. There were no boundaries. I searched, as my mother, for the pain and some understanding of this illness. She wanted answers and so did I. When I finished Bev that night, I wanted to stay still and weep, but I had to go on with the show.

By Wednesday night, after incarnating her twice, I was ready for the psychiatric ward myself. I could feel the Haldol, a new improved version of Thorazine, racing through my own veins.

When I got home, I had this message on the answering machine: "Hello, my baby. Well, Sherry, if you think Pee Wee had a big adventure, you should see me. *Hahahahaha.*" Click.

I called my father. He sounded exhausted. He had had no sleep the previous night and this one looked to be just as long. I spoke to my brother. They were preparing for the onslaught of well-meaning friends and relatives to gently coax my mother into reality. They all did their best, suggesting she take some lithium and get back on track. She didn't think there was anything wrong with her. But she had promised all of us that, after she came off lithium if any of the people who loved her, especially me or my father or my brother, said she was off and needed to take lithium again, she would. But when she is high, promises mean nothing.

family secrets

She was preparing to do a show for everyone. She had dressed up in an outfit of shimmering silk and dramatic high heels and was ready to perform when my father again suggested she take her medicine.

"How many do you want me to take?" she asked him.

"Three."

"And, Steven, how many do you want me to take?"

"I want you to take three, Mom."

"And Linda, how about you?"

"Three, Aunt Shelly." She asked everyone in the room. Three was the answer.

"Okay." She said, "Three, six, nine, twelve. Hell, I'll take the whole bottle." She went to the counter and opened the bottle and dumped the pills in her mouth. This was my father's cue. The only way he could get her committed to the hospital was if she was destroying someone's property, she was a threat to some-one else, or she was suicidal. She had no intention of actually swallowing those pills, but it was good enough for my father. He called the police.

Dad had also made special arrangements with the doctor at Garden Pavilion to take my mother in under these circum-stances. Being affluent and having good connections in the community served him well at this point. They could hold her for seventy-two hours there, under special circumstances and hopefully by then she would have seen the light and come down to earth. He called the hospital to tell them she would be com-ing in shortly, but the doctor had gone home and left no specific instructions about the arrangement. My father was panicky.

The police arrived and tried to assess the situation. My mother invited them in and offered to do a tarot reading for them, but not before guessing their astrological signs. She was correct, but that did not exactly help her cause. They were soon convinced that she was not in touch with reality as they knew it. They were going to take her to Salinas. My father convinced

sherry glaser ✳

them that he had a special agreement with Community Hospital. He finally got the doctor on the phone and he assured them it was true.

My mother, however, was not interested in going to the hospital. She wanted to have a party. The police handcuffed her and put her in the patrol car. Everyone stood by in stony silence and wrenching pain. My father especially. My mother had enough wits about her to know she didn't want to be in a police car alone, in this state. She said, "I want my mother to go with me." Her dearest friend climbed into the car and accompanied her to the hospital. They admitted her, drugged her, and tied her to the bed, while she sang songs from *The Sound of Music.*

My father called me and told me what happened. He was in tears. I apologized for supporting her decision to go off lithium. He was right. I hated saying it, but I had to. I was humiliated, embarrassed that I had been the only one who believed that she had truly healed herself, that one *could* heal something like that. I felt stupid. I felt like a little kid, so I said I was sorry. My father said it wasn't my fault and he loved me, but I could hear some righteousness in the forgiveness. At least I thought I did. He and my brother were going to sleep. They were in desperate need of rest. Tomorrow would be better, my father told me. "We have to go on. She's on her own path." He was quoting my mother.

The next day I felt distant from myself. Trying to unite with her in my mind, I would hold her and kiss her and say, "Please, come back, Mom." Shelly had been calling lawyers and trying to get herself out. She was taking her medication and talking on the phone a lot. She called her friends and told them what was being done to her because of my father's wishes. It was a tug of war, and still my show went on. On Saturday, when my father and brother went to visit my mother, she sidled up to my father as if to whisper something in his ear and bit him. She bit him hard. When he told me this on Saturday night, I was finished. I

family secrets

couldn't function. I couldn't imagine having to get on stage, yet again and become her. I hated her. I hated what she was doing.

Greg told me to cancel the show. It was a Sunday. It was sold out. How could I cancel the show? I never cancel shows unless I'm dropping dead or I have absolutely no voice, which had happened only twice in my New York run.

I called my manager, who had also been my good friend for years. She had been apprised of the situation all along. She said, "Do you want to cancel the show?"

I said, "I don't feel like I'm capable of making a decision right now. I don't know what to do."

She said, "Okay, sleep on it and call me in the morning when you wake up so I can let the company manager know in time and we can call as many people as possible." I cried myself to sleep.

I called Irene in the morning. She had canceled the show. I was grateful. I got to take care of myself, lick my wounds, and spend time with my daughter. I needed to feel safe, unexposed, and I was relieved not to have to be my mother.

By Monday my mother was back in earth's atmosphere—not on the ground, but surely plummeting this way. I finally spoke to her on the phone. She sounded sad, hurt, tired from all the medication. She wanted to go home. She was taking the lithium and agreed that she would continue to do so, but she wanted to go home. Everybody else wanted her to stay and do some more jigsaw puzzles and throw clay pots, but the therapy she longed for was not available at this hospital. It was more of a control situation, no provision for real introspection and healing. She had a hearing arranged with the hospital board for the next day and she went home.

My father was nervous about her being home, but there was nothing he could do. It was her choice, and he called upon the kindness and company of those who loved her again, to visit with her while he went to work for the first couple of days. She and I talked a lot.

My mother was incredibly wise and stoic about the results of her failed experiment. She said, "I learned an important lesson. I had to know what would happen if I got off it and I found out. I had emotionally healed the trauma of my life, but I hadn't dealt with the chemical imbalance. I have to wait for my body to heal as well as my emotions. But I'm not going to do anything about it for a long time. I need to let my body rest. I put it through hell and I'm tired. I'm really tired."

She said, "You were the only one who supported me in this decision and I thank you so much for that. Even though it didn't turn out the way we had hoped, you trusted me in it. Thank you. I'm sorry you got hurt and everybody got so upset, but you know, Sher, it wasn't all bad. Those first couple of days we had a ball. Steven was here and we made fritatta and we laughed a lot."

I learned two very important things from this episode as well. First, I still have work to do with the psychic boundaries of my mother. Even though I become her, I need to have a safety zone that exists when her real life becomes unbearable to me. I need to be compassionate to her, but not abandon my own life to save her. Second, I learned more about pain. The night that she bit my father, the pain in my body was so extreme I felt as if I would explode. In retrospect I don't think I should have canceled the show. I artificially delivered myself through the pain, sort of like a C-section. Since I did that I haven't been able to totally immerse myself in Bev. I think I should have stayed with the pain, drowned in it, and come through the other side. In other words I'm not done with it. As my mother is still healing, so am I.

I had a fantasy that I would arrive in New York and the Oceanside High School class of 1978 would buy out a night at the theater and surprise me and then have a party honoring me to make up for my lost invitation to the ten-year high school reunion. At this personal gala I would reunite with the lost boys and girls and we would confront and forgive and laugh and cry at the terrible and dangerous games we played at each other's and our own bodies' expense.

It didn't happen. (Heidi Askenazy came and was absolutely thrilled to have her name used in the show and we have since rekindled our timeless friendship.)

I looked up my old friend Peter from high school. I got in touch with him through a girlfriend who had read about me in *Newsday*. He and Kenny decided to come in late summer; they had been best friends with David. I was really nervous about their presence. They might know who Sandra was talking about and the many sexual compromises I had made. Sandra was extra painful that night.

I know, here I am thirty-four years old. High school was over fifteen years ago, but still I had self-esteem problems that dated back to age sixteen. In performing the show in front of my peers I was revealing the raw and real insecurities about myself that still plagued me—the way I look, the burden of time and childbirth on my hips, and my always challenging relationship with my beauty or lack thereof. Sandra is my ongoing struggle to accept myself as a beautiful woman, strong, full-bodied with distinguished and bold features.

One evening the American Association of Bulimics and Anorexics held a benefit at the theater. I was asked to speak afterward and answer questions. After a brief session, the director of the association came on the stage and presented me with an award for being the 1994 Powerful Role Model for Women. Though I'd won the L.A. Critics award and the Theaterworld award for "Outstanding Debut in New York Theater," this award meant the most to me.

My daughter is seven years old. Reliving her birth every evening, 458 times on the New York stage, was the most demanding of all. The physical exertion is unparalleled; in the beginning I had to go to the chiropractor twice a week, just to be able to move without terrible back pain. But it's the emotional drama of it that drains me most.

Our lives have been a series of short stays in wonderful places. We've never really had a home. After spending a year in New York, Greg and Dana were tired of the noise and the cement and longed for California. Our original agreement was that I would only stay one year. The show's success prompted a three-month extension, and I couldn't ask them to stay any longer, so they went back to California, to our home in Mendocino County, land of the redwoods. Being separated from them was horrible. I hated it. I hated not seeing Dana, smelling her, kissing the bridge of her nose. When she gets sick I hate not being there to bring her back to health with my magic bags of herbs and crystals.

One night I got home from the theater to find a disturbing message on the answering machine from Gregory.

"Honey, Dana's all right, but we had a bit of a crisis." Oh no. My heart fell into my boots. "She and Larissa were outside on the roof and Dana fell off. She's okay."

Just that morning I was in the shower and I had one of those nasty little chills go down my spine, like something terrible had happened. I thought Dana was hurt, or possibly killed. I dismissed it saying to myself for the hundredth time, "Will you stop being so paranoid? She's fine. She's going to have a long and healthy life, and even if she isn't, there is no use worrying about it. Let her go, she's on her own path."

I called Greg back immediately. "What happened? Is she okay? Why was she on the roof?" It seems that she and Larissa had developed the dangerous habit of peeing off the roof. We don't have a bathroom in the woods, we have an outhouse. The girls were too lazy to go downstairs and outside to pee, so they did it off the roof. Greg had warned them not to do this, but be-

⬛ family secrets

ing seven years old, they knew better. Dana had squatted, lost her balance, and tumbled down eight feet to the hard soil below. She landed on her feet. Greg was sure that angels had guided her down, because barely one foot away from her was a menacing pile of jagged and very hard redwood. I asked to speak to her.

"Hi, Dana, I love you. I'm so glad you're okay. So, how are you?"

"I'm a little sore," she said.

"Did you learn anything from the experience?" I asked.

"I learned that I'm never gonna do that again."

"Good," I said. "How did it feel to fall like that?"

"Well," she said, "at first I thought I would smack into the ground right away, but then I opened my eyes and I saw I had a long way to go."

Three days later she wrote this poem.

> When I fell
> when I hit the bottom
> I had tears
> I thought that it would teach me a lesson and it did.
> When I fell, fell in tears
> But this on the other side
> It was quite beautiful to see me fall.

Because of our crazy living situation she has flown back and forth across the country a couple of times by herself. It is always her idea and she bravely boards the plane with her backpack stuffed with nutritious and gooey goodies from me. It happened that she would usually fly on a matinee day and actually be up in the air when I was in the midst of Kahari. When I got to the line: "I grew to love this baby more than I've ever loved anybody in my whole life, and sometimes it's so much that I can't bear it, because I'm afraid something might happen to her," I would just bawl my little eyes out. It's a deep and cavernous love for this one I have. I had no idea.

sherry glaser ✄

On May 2, 1995, I was performing in Chicago as part of a six-month tour following my New York engagement. At seven forty-five that morning I got a call from my father. He said my grandmother had died. He was crying. Hearing my father cry makes me cry. The only other time I remember it happening was when his father died. I know his cry was sorrowful, but I could clearly hear the relief. My grandmother had been dying for years and years. I cried too. For the death of potential, for the break in connection, for my own step closer to mortality, for the love I never felt.

It was a Tuesday and I had to perform that night. I wasn't sure if I was going to fly home for the funeral. I would have to miss performances. Why should I go? What was the point? Did I feel any love for my grandmother other than the obligatory bindings of blood?

I look mostly like my grandmother. Big brown eyes, whose expressions lean toward sad. My hair is the rich chestnut brown that she sported in her youth. And we both have very large breasts.

On the day I was born, my grandmother Rose stuck her head out the window of the hospital and hollered for all the Bronx to hear that she had a girl. She had desperately wanted a girl of her own, but got four boys. Of course I wasn't *her* girl, but my father was hers and hence I was too. It would take many years before she would let go of the property rights to her son and his offspring.

My grandmother was good with babies, at least talking with them. Her ability to babble and coo were unparalleled. She could play hide and seek for hours and *cootchie-coo* and *wooda wooda wooda wooda pweety widdle giwl*. But when it came to having conversations, as one grew up there was nothing. She could only ask, "So what's new?" "So, nothing's new?" "So what's doin' with you?" She wanted to be entertained, a one-way grandma.

family secrets

When it was time to go to Grandma's house I would cry. I hated it. It smelled terrible, like urine, because of her early incontinence and the alcohol my grandfather used to consume as his daily diet. I didn't mind visiting her at work. She worked at Barton's, the best candy store in New York City. That's the only reason I ever wanted to see her. Because she gave me chocolate. I loved chocolate, especially the fabulous chocolate-covered raisins that Barton's specialized in. Grandma would give me a bagful of those and I would give her a kiss.

For twenty years my grandmother lived in the Bronx with my grandfather and her youngest son, born nineteen years after my father and five years before me. My grandfather was a small and wrinkly old man. I don't suppose he was more than fifty-five, but he looked like he was seventy-five. When I visited them, he liked me to sit on his lap and he would breathe in my face. His jowls were unshaven and his breath unbearable, but I was a good little girl and I would stay as long as I could stand it and not upset him or hurt his feelings.

When I was seven years old I came home from school and my mother had been crying. I got scared. "Mommy what's wrong?"

"Grandpa died," she said. I was relieved. I'm not sure if he did anything to hurt me directly—my memory isn't that good—but I was glad never to have to sit on his lap again.

Rose Stein was born the oldest of four on September 19, 1910. Her mother died of lobar pneumonia when she was nine and some sadistic soul made her stay up with the open coffin all night. Her marriage was loveless. Her first child, Edward, died in his crib. I had very little compassion for her, because her suffering was eternal.

There she is, the lovely old woman sitting in her rocking chair, knitting a delightful sparkling wool cardigan. Knit one, purl two. She smells of sugar and butter and vanilla and maybe a touch of gardenia. I am at her knee looking through a photo album of her younger days. She is telling me stories of all the gay

sherry glaser ⚡

places she frequented and the young men who courted her and the handsome, yet troublesome one that finally conquered her heart. This is a dream. This is a TV movie. This is not my grandma.

I longed for her to be this Hallmark rendition of a granny, but I got a spoiled version, a disappointing substitute. I got Grandma Rose. My grandmother suffered through her life, didn't know she had any other choice. Her suffering made her unable to love, or be hopeful, to share, to be anything but miserable. She denied having any needs, but turned out to be the grandest leech of all. She gave everything to her children, so she had and was nothing. She behaved as though she didn't matter and it was our job to make her matter. She had so many opportunities for joy, for love, but she was blind to them and essentially found joy, or at least comfort in misery. She was so sick and unhappy for so long that we all expected her to die twenty years earlier, but she kept on living through two suicide attempts, quadruple bypass surgery, and double pneumonia, not to mention falls and accidents galore. She shoplifted, hitchhiked on the freeway. She was a riot.

My father called us in Fort Lauderdale two years ago to tell us that it looked like my grandmother was on her last leg. She had fluid in her lungs and the doctors were giving a dim prognosis. I told him I was sorry for him and I was relieved that her suffering would be over. I hung up and told Greg what he had said. "Well, how do you feel about that?" he asked.

I had to stop and think about it. I said, "Well, I feel sad, mostly for my father, and for myself I feel a bit guilty."

"Why?" he asked.

"Because the last thing I said to her when I saw her in September was, 'I'll call you,' and I never did. So I feel guilty."

He said, "She wouldn't have it any other way."

Last time I saw her was in a nursing home. My father and I went to visit her. She recognized him and he told her that he had brought Sheryl, her granddaughter. I was standing right next to him. She said, "Good, where is she?"

I said, "I'm standing right here."

She said, "You're not Sheryl."

I said, "Yes, I am."

She said, "I don't like your hair."

I wrestled with the idea of going to the funeral. I'd have to fly a long way and cancel at least one show, maybe two. I had to decide quickly for the sake of the ticket buyers. I wanted to go for selfish reasons. For the material, for the chance to see the family in action. I'd never been to a funeral and I wanted to say good-bye to Rose. I wanted to pay my respects to my father. I wanted to be there for him. I made a reservation for the next morning at nine and got the airline's bereavement discount.

My father called again around noon from the car phone. They had been driving around all afternoon trying to find a place to bury her. It seemed the cemetery's schedule was booked and they'd have to wait until Friday rather than Thursday (the only day I could reasonably attend) to have the funeral. This actually interfered with a lot of the family's scheduling. So my mother called on her magic powers. She asked her automatic writing to tell her why they were having such a hard time burying Mom. The writing responded: "Mom doesn't want to be buried in that old dress." It did seem possible. My father had grabbed a drab old green dress out of a box from the garage. My parents drove to Macy's. My mother found a beautiful white lace dress with little red rose buttons, the perfect size. The tag said "Wild Rose." She found soft satin slippers to match. They drove over to the funeral home and had the mortician redress her. They got back on the phone to recheck the cemeteries and easily got an appointment for Thursday at 2 P.M.

When I transformed into Rose that evening, singing, "As

Time Goes By," I was walloped by the emotion. My voice cracked and I had to pause for a couple of minutes in order to continue with any sound at all. And it wasn't really me there on that stage in her costume. It felt as though she had come . . . through spirit, and for a moment put on the life I had created for her. I felt her joy and excitement to be living a life full of hope and joy and love, and that made me weep. Following the performance I announced to the audience that Rose had died that morning and I was dedicating the show to her. I could hear them crying too.

I left my apartment at seven the next morning to make it to O'Hare for a nine o'clock flight to get to a two o'clock funeral in California. After a harrowing journey that included canceled flights and last-minute rerouting, I was picked up by my brother at the Monterey airport. We both agreed that our sadness was not about losing our grandmother but our immense love and sympathy for our father. We arrived at the house to find the family in solemn funeral attire and listening to marvelous stories of Rose, told by her little brother, Joe, now seventy-five.

My father actually seemed okay. He had been dealing with his grief beautifully, and it was especially helpful to have the rabbi come the previous evening and listen to my father and his brothers reminisce about their mother's life. My mother was the one who seemed undone. She was coming to terms with her grief, because even though Rose wasn't her mother and was a conniving and selfish mother-in-law, she was still the only mother figure she had had for most of her life. My mother and I let the others go ahead while I waited behind and let her cry in my arms.

When the rabbi spoke of my grandmother as she lay in the simple pine casket before us, he made all her faults sound like virtues. He spoke of her sacrifices so her children could be happy, her strength in getting things she wanted, her will to live and go on under the most difficult circumstances. As he spoke, I

family secrets

looked up through the skylight of the temple and saw a hawk hovering overhead for the longest time.

Afterward, the rabbi invited whoever wanted to view the body to stay. I did. I stood with my father, mother, brother, and uncle and watched as the rabbi lifted the lid. There she was in her pretty white dress. I touched her hands. They were freezing, empty. The plump, miserable little old lady was now gaunt and sallow and at peace.

Capturing my grandmother's character requires a physical marathon. The jutting chin, the loose dentures, the crooked hands and hunched back seem like a harsh forecast of my future. But I look at the stunning octa- and nonagenarians in my audience and I see their straight backs and lucid expressions. They have taken care of themselves, they have come through the storm and stand like glorious oaks. If I live my life with integrity and continue to confront the still rising sorrows and torments, I too will stand up straight for a long, long time.

When I reach the grandmother in the show I know I am nearly finished. It is a relief when I arrive at her character, because for most of it I can sit down, and by this point I have created such warmth and intimacy in the room it's like cuddling up under a warm quilt. I sit in her chair, a shrunken replica of myself, and I speak of love.

> You must remember this, a kiss is just a kiss a sigh is but a sigh
> The fundamental things apply as time goes by.

> *(Transforms into* ROSE. *First red checkered pants go on, followed by matching blouse. While singing, she sits at vanity, with head facing down, puts on wig and glasses, voice changes to* ROSE *and looks up. "As Time Goes By" continues to play.)*

> *(She rises very slowly and looks at audience.)*

sherry glaser ⚹

Hava Nagila, Hava Nagila
Hava Nagila
Vey nis micha
Sing along. Come on everybody.

Hava Nagila. . . . *(waits)*
Aren't you all Jewish?
Do you know what a "nagila" is?

I'll tell you.
A long time ago in Israel, when a woman of the house
would have guests over, she would greet them at the door
with a plate of flaky pastry called nagila.
She would say, "Hello, hava nagila."

I love that song.
I never hear it on the radio.
Maybe it's an old song. Maybe I'm an old lady.
But look at you. *(She looks at someone in the front row.)*

You're gorgeous, gorgeous, gorgeous.
I could bite your tushy.

I used to be gorgeous. Not no more.
No my face is all fashmutz and my boobs are all saggy.
And I got gas. I got awful gas.
Just this morning Milton was in the shower and I was in
the living room and I farted and he said, "What did you
say Rose?"

(She shuffles over to chair.)

I got old. I don't know when I got old.
I think it was two weeks ago.
No, I know when it happened.
When I retired from the post office in New York.
I felt used up, worn out.

family secrets

My husband was gone and Mort moved to California.
I had nobody, nobody.
I went to sisterhood, I played Mah Jong.
But I was lonely.
So one night I took half a bottle of aspirin and then I
stuck my head in the oven.

Mrs. Lippman smelled the gas, she ran, got the super.
They're banging on my door.
I said, "I got a right to die."
But they took me to the hospital.
Mort called me there.
He said, "Ma, what happened?"
I said, "I tried to kill myself."
He said, "Ma, you live on the thirty-third floor. Why
didn't you just jump out the window?"
I couldn't believe he said that to me.
I said, "It's too cold."
He said, "Why don't you come out to California? It's nice
all year long."

So I moved here and that's how I met Milton.
I met him at a senior citizen luncheon.
We're sitting at the same table and he's telling jokes, awful
jokes.
He said, "What's a dentist's favorite song?"
"I don't know, I don't know."
"Fillings . . . nothing more than fillings."

Well, I was the only one laughing, so he asked me out and
he took me to *Pee-wee's Big Adventure.*
I thought the picture was silly, but he loved it.
He laughed the whole time. He looked like a little boy.
That's when I fell in love.

sherry glaser ☒

So we started spending every day together and eventually,
every night together.
Yes, we are sexually active,
but it's nothing like the movies.
With us sex is awkward.

"Hey, you're on my hair. Could you get off a minute? I
can't breathe."
And sometimes he's all hot and heavy and I'm thinking,
"Did I pay the insurance bill this month?"
Well, you know your mind wanders.
But he knows, he knows right away and he says,
"Rose, where are you?"
And I say, "Rose isn't here right now, but I can take a
message."
And we laugh and we fall asleep holding each other like
friends.
We're friends, right? Right.

For a while I was afraid.
I said, "Milton, we're having too much sex. One of us is
gonna have a heart attack."
He said, "What's the matter, Rose? Are you afraid to
die?"
I said, "Yes, now that I got you."
He said, "Well, what do you want to do? You want to
stare out the window?
Sit in your rockin' chair and be bored to death? Or you
want to go out with me and live it up and just drop
dead?"
Well, he had a point.
So we started playing racquetball.
Oh, we don't compete. We're just very glad when the
other one gets to the ball.

▪ family secrets

And we go dancing and we go out to dinner all the time.
He's always gotta order dessert.
He says, "Life should be sweet."
He's a nice man.

One time we were out to dinner, I don't know what happened, but I wet my pants.
I was so embarrassed and upset, of course.
And he said, "Rose, what's wrong?"
I said, "Milton, I wet my pants."
He said, "I didn't know you were having such a good time."
"No," I said, "I had an accident. I lost control."
He said, "Oh, okay."
He paid the bill and he got up and he pulled my chair out for me.
So when I stood up no one could see.
(She gets up with difficulty.)

Then he put his arms around me and he walked out of the restaurant like that.
Saying in my ear, "I love you, Rose. You're beautiful.
You're just a big baby, that's all."
I never felt so loved in my whole life.
And a couple of days later he asked me to marry him.
I said, "Marry you? What do you want to marry me for?
I'm an old woman. I'm fallin' apart."
He said, "Rose, I want to make an honest woman out of you and I want you to have my baby."
He's a nut. He's a nut.
But I married him anyway.

We got married at the La Jolla Bridge and Shuffleboard Club,
right on the coast.

sherry glaser ■

Beautiful day.
We had a band and we had a gefilte fish swan.
Delicious.

And my whole family was there.
My children and my children's children and their children
and
I could see a little schmutz of me in all of them.
And I always wanted someone to sing this song at my
wedding, but I sang it.
(She sings the first verse of "Sunrise, Sunset.")
Sing along.

Sunrise, boom . . . Sunset.
Sunrise . . . boom . . . Sunset.

You are all Jewish.

It was a wonderful wedding.
We sang and we danced and then there was a fight.
Well, Mort said something to Miguel.
I don't know what he said, but Fern was crying in the
bathroom and Bev was yelling at Mort.
Everybody was screaming. Screaming.
And then we had cake.

Well, that's family.
And no matter what you do you can't rid of them.
My father is dead fifty years, but I can still hear his voice
in my head.
"Rose, if you can type, you'll always have something to
fall back on."
I'll always be his daughter and Mort will always be my
baby.
And Fern and Sandra and Joel will always be his children.
We're family.

family secrets

And if we didn't have families we'd all be strangers.
Like when you came in tonight, we were strangers, now
we're like family.
So next year, ya come to me for Passover.

Good night, Good night.

Reliving my life on stage for the past decade has offered me unparalleled insight, for which I am grateful. Seeing the choices I have made, the confrontations I have initiated, the icons I have smashed and replaced has led me to a consistent, conscious, and healthy life. I am in touch with my value, my talent, and my strength and beauty. Sure, I still struggle, like any human being. I fight with my husband and wonder if home-schooling my daughter will handicap her. I occasionally look in the mirror and criticize my belly. I still like a cigarette now and then, and my mother can still drive me crazy, but I have reliable, creative tools to deal with the worry and the pain. I'll just put it in a show; maybe even the sequel to *Family Secrets—Family Reunion*.

By the conclusion of the show, those who have come in skeptical or downhearted have been lifted and inspired and they sing with me. "Is this the little girl I carried . . . Is this the little boy at play? I don't remember growing older, when did they?" They have been moved, touched by the honesty and the courage of this awkward, funny, simple family. This is my family. This is my story and as far as I know, we all lived happily ever after.